LIVE-ABOARD
THE ESSENTIAL GUIDE
DIVE TRAVEL

Dear Monica,

Looking forward to diving with you on a live-aboard!

Love,

Your Godfather,
Wujek Rysiu

A Best Publication

LIVE-ABOARD
THE ESSENTIAL GUIDE
DIVE TRAVEL

Astrid Witte
Capt. Casey Mahaney

A Best Publication

ISBN: 0-941332-54-3
Library of Congress catalog card number: 96-084464

Composed, printed and bound in the United States of America.

Best Publishing Company
2355 North Steves Boulevard
P.O. Box 30100
Flagstaff, Arizona 86003-0100 USA

TABLE OF CONTENTS

Acknowledgements ix
Introduction. xi
How to Read This Book. xiii
A Historical Account of Live-Aboard Diving 1
Live-Aboard Advantages over Shore Based Diving. 7
Mothership Diving and Advanced Skills. 9
Drift Diving. 20
Buddy System 30
Dive Equipment Considerations 34
Reef Conservation and Marine Life 43
Underwater Photography 50
Additional Live-Aboard Tips and Etiquette 63
Communications 67
Seasickness 69
Meals Aboard 72
Packing 74
Live-Aboard Selection 81
Choosing The Right Destination 89
Destinations: Definitions of Terms 93
Bahamas 99
Bay Islands of Honduras 102
Belize 104
Cayman Islands 106
Turks & Caicos 108
Coco Island, Costa Rica 110
Galapagos 113
Kona Coast/Island of Hawaii 116
Fiji Islands 119
Indonesia 122
Papua New Guinea 125
The Great Barrier Reef/Coral Sea 128
Solomon Islands 131
Palau (Belau), Micronesia 134
Truk Lagoon (Chuuk), Micronesia 137
Booking Your Trip 140
Contact Information for : 148
    Dive Travel Agents 148
    Direct Booking Information 149
    Professional Tour Leaders 151
    Airlines 154
Arrival and Departure 155
Insurance 158
Gratuities 160

About the Authors

Astrid Witte and Casey Mahaney

Our combined 19 years of experience in the dive industry include:

- Captain and instructor aboard the Cayman, Truk, Kona Aggressor and Spirit of Solomons (Bilikiki Cruises)
- Authors and photographers of: HAWAIIAN REEF FISH The Identification Book and THE REEF WATCHERS I.D. Series for Hawaii, Guam and Micronesia
- Over 1200 SCUBA Certifications
- Organization and guiding of Live-Aboard dive tours world wide
- Publications in many international dive and adventure travel journals
- Dive shop owner and operator

Since 1989 we've averaged over thirty weeks each year, as either captain, tour leader, instructor, photo pro, cook and engineer on Live -Aboard dive yachts, and, over the years, have seen the problems which occur with divers that have been either misinformed about Live-Aboards in general or about the destination itself, or simply arrived with no information pass their initial open water SCUBA certification. We feel that by sharing our accumulated knowledge and experiences with you, we can greatly enhance your first or next Live-Aboard dive experience.

Although we have gained a great deal of our experience aboard Aggressor Fleet vessels, this guide is in no way promoting any one operation associated or not associated with the Aggressor Fleet. We, as authors, are under no obligation to any organization within the dive industry at the time of this writing.

We hope you enjoy Live-Aboard diving as much as we do.

Astrid & Casey

ACKNOWLEDGEMENTS

This guide was inspired by the questions most divers have about Live-Aboard dive travel. With the advent of on-line SCUBA forums we came to realize that most divers needed an additional source to base their travel decisions. We would like to thank all the divers we have had the pleasure to work with over the years.

As with all books, this publication came together with the assistance of a great number of individuals. We would specifically like to thank Chris Newbert and Birgitte Wilms, Jim Watt, Jim Church, Ann Fielding, Mike and Pauline Severns, Mark Bernardi, Doug Perrine, Jack Randall and Tom Campbell, who took the time to help us out with specific destination information.

We would also like to thank the operators of the Nai'a, Bilikiki Cruises, Reef Explorer, MV Ballymena, Aggressor Fleet and Peter Hughes Diving, who answered a variety of detailed questions, as well as Evin Cotter, Jacky Dallas and Dan Ruth from the office of Live/Dive Pacific, who generously helped us out with many aspects.

A special thanks goes out to Stan Waterman who was kind enough to take the time to give us a personal account of his own Live-Aboard history.

Photocredit:
Front Cover: Top-courtesy of Nai'a Cruises
Middle-Casey Mahaney/Astrid Witte
Bottom-courtesy of Live/Dive Pacific

Back Cover: Top-Casey Mahaney/Astrid Witte
Middle-Casey Mahaney/Astrid Witte
Bottom-courtesy of Live/Dive Pacific

Clipart provided by: *Divers Art Disk* by P.S.L. and Debbie Reese

Schematic provided by: Peter Hughes Diving

INTRODUCTION

The Live-Aboard craze is here, and here to stay. Many seasoned divers and top professionals in the dive industry have discovered the comfort and convenience Live-Aboards offer, and now do most, if not all, their diving from Live Aboards There is no question about the many advantages a vessel, emulating a hotel, restaurant and dive facility, can present for all types of divers. With the explosion of this new trend has come the need for 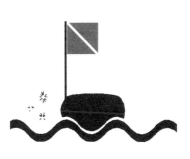 this guide to provide you with the information for thorough preparation.

As experienced captain, instructors and tourleaders on Live-Aboards, we have noticed that far too often divers arrive in a destination extremely ill prepared and unknowledgeable of the true diving conditions, or have unrealistic expectations of the weather, or marine life they will encounter.

We have dedicated this guide to give divers a realistic and clear overview of the Live-Aboard industry and some of the most popular world class diving destinations. The information and tips on advanced dive skills we provide, would take most divers years to acquire. We explain critical details to make diving on Live-Aboards safer, easier and more fun. This book will give you fundamental knowledge about underwater photography, marine life conservation, drift diving in strong currents and basic mothership diving, along with much much more.

We let the operator's brochures tell you about their underwater beauty, their amenities, food or service on their specific vessel. Since cooks, crew, captains and owners change, consistency is difficult to achieve month after month. It is our intention to assist you, the discriminating diver, with factual information so you can make your own well prepared decisions.

How to read this book

The beginning chapters introduce you to different types of Live-Aboard set ups, advanced diving skills, different diving styles and equipment considerations.

We recommend, that you read *"Selection of a Live-Aboard"* in combination with the operator's brochure and/or the books "Live Aboards of the World" and "Asia Pacific Live-Aboards." Together these books describe more than 100 Live-Aboards in detail.

"Choosing your destination" helps you narrow down your choices according to your experience level and priorities.

"Destinations: Definitions of Terms" is designed to be read before studying each destination chapter, and referred back to, whenever you need a detailed explanation of a specific term.

"Booking your trip" explains your options of booking your entire trip, along with phone numbers, addresses of Live-Aboard operators, wholesalers and professional tour leaders as well as airlines.

A Historical Account of Live-Aboard Diving
By Stan Waterman

Now with over 150 Live-Aboards plying the world's oceans, providing an accurate and up-to-date historical account of every operation would be a monumental task. Since there is no official date or specific occurrence that signifies the "birth" of Live-Aboard diving, we have found the following account of Stan Waterman's personal experience and observations over the many years to give us an overview of how this industry has developed.

I should start at the first Live-Aboard that I spent a week on. The year was 1971. The boat was a hard-worn, retired, wooden-hulled WWII mine sweeper. It was named the *Cayman Diver* and it was owned, fitted and operated by a lawyer who decided he didn't want to spend the rest of his life bilking widows and orphans. His name was (and is) Paul Humann. Introducing Paul Humann is much like introducing the father of our country as a little boy, caught cutting down a cherry tree, who was destined to become our first president. Paul is, of course, perhaps the most prestigious and popular authority on fish identification today. His reference books are visible in any dive activity in the U.S. and Canada and on Live-Aboards from the Galapagos to the Bahamas.

At any rate, and as I was saying when I was side tracked by introducing Paul, he made a break from the law and the bible belt to the diving world at a time, when that took far more imagination and risk than it does today. The first *Cayman Diver* was a dog. The forward hold, where the bunks were tiered deep on either side, was a black hole that rustled with roach traffic in the still of night. It was so damp that all dunnage was clothed with a fur coat of mold in a day. Paul did the cooking. That was world-class, Paul being a formidable gourmet himself. Frankly, I can't remember the diving. I do remember that the novelty of not having to shuttle back and forth from a shore resort pleased us all.

1

We logged more diving in one week than others at resorts could compound in a month.

When launched in November 1984, the first *Cayman Aggressor* amazed and delighted all of us who had cut our teeth on the first motley array of Live-Aboards. It set a standard that has served generally as a guide for the gradually improving Live-Aboard that would come off the ways in the next years.

There were hot-water showers, and clean heads below. The dive deck had rows of tanks on either side that backed on commodious bench seats in which were individual lockers for each person's gear. In the center was a large felt covered table for the cameras. Broad ladders at the stern on either side led down to the dive platform of which you simply stepped off to start your dive. Tanks were filled and replaced at the divers station. Wet suits were hung up to dry. It was a SCUBA assembly line making possible as many as five dives a day. The boat moved from location to location, depending on the wind and weather; so you were always over the dive site. When you

returned from your dive there was a crewman on the dive platform to help you up with your fins, camera, etc., fresh-water rinse tank for cameras, freshwater showers at the stern were available for an immediate rinse off. Hot, fresh towels were stacked at hand and a stewardess passed with hot muffins and goodies. An upper deck provided lounges for warming in the sun and getting brown. It was a bit much. We were spoiled rotten. It took no protean mind to realize that if it was diving you wanted, the Live-Aboard had it at its best.

Improvements over the years were generally created with that basic structure. And then there were two, when the second *Cayman Aggressor* was launched. In time, the two became a fleet that stretched to other parts of the Caribbean, (Belize, Antilles and Bay Islands). Each new Aggressor was an improvement over the first and modifications were effected, too, when the boats went into dry dock periodically.

In 1988 Aggressor Fleet granted their first franchise to Live/Dive Pacific for a Live-Aboard operation in Kona, Hawaii. This franchise was followed by ones in Costa Rica (*Okeanos Aggressor*), Truk Lagoon, Palau and Galapagos.

All this while Peter Hughes launched his own fleet of excellent Live-Aboards and named them the *Dancers*. First came the *Sea Dancer*, followed by the *Wave Dancer*, *Sun Dancer* and the recent *Wind Dancer*.

For those who are not familiar with the Aggressor Fleet and the fleets of fine Live-Aboards developed by Peter Hughes, I would explain that these two fleets were started by two highly competitive and able divemasters at a time when Live-Aboards were a motley collection of superannuated and modified commercial vessels and private yachts. I knew both of the progenitors of these fleets when they were divemasters. Now they are both in the diving world, as successful and proud, as the Greek owners of the great merchant fleets.

Wayne Hasson was a divemaster at *Casa Bertmar*, a small resort on the island of Grand Cayman. He achieved early notoriety as the friend of the giant moray eel, Waldo, with whom he carried on like Lida and the swan. I met him early on while producing a P.R. film for Cayman Airways. Wayne and Waldo were a must, a jewel in the crown of Grand Cayman diving, like Tarpon Alley and Stingray City, which hadn't been developed yet.

I met Peter Hughes when he was a divemaster at Anthony's Key Club on Roatan Island. I remember, he was dark and fierce looking, Hollywood would have cast him on the spot as a pirate captain. When I next met him, Peter was the director of the diving activities at a resort on Grand Cayman, called _Spanish Cove_. The resort had been recently purchased by a John MacMillion, a name that was most apocryphal for a giant in the pipe line business. When MacMillion added _Casa Bertmar_ to his properties, Peter Hughes assumed direction of the diving there, thus replacing Wayne and his future wife, Ann, with his own team.

I have rather thought that the seeds of vigorous competition between the two men may have been sown at that time.

How often what seems like adverse fortune that causes a person to change course turns out to be the beginning of a bright future. So it turned out for Wayne. In the early 80s an oil glut had dried up the market for US produced oil. At a ship yard in Morgan City, LA, the hull of a 90 foot crew boat remained unfinished and unwanted. A serendipitous partnership between Wayne, the seasoned and popular divemaster, and Paul Haines, owner of the shipyard, plus a Grand Caymanian silent partner, was the genesis for the first _Cayman Aggressor_.

As I write this remembrance of times past, I am actually on my forth _Palau Aggressor_ trip. I can describe the _Palau Aggressor II_ through intimate use. It is arguably the most advanced, most comfortable, most diver friendly and thoughtfully engineered Live-Aboard in the world today. In a history of the development of Live-Aboards, it may serve as an example of the level to which that development has arrived. This twin aluminum hulled ship has a length of 106' with a 30' beam and a draft of only 4.5'. It is three decks high and so stands off the water with a rather boxy appearance. A sleek clipper-like hull it is not. It is built for stability and comfort, something of a floating hotel. However, with two CAT Diesel 1050 hp jet engines, it cruises easily at 21 knots; and with its shallow draft can cozy up to dive areas too shallow for most dive boats. The _piece de resistance_ is the 30' dive skiff that is boarded at the cabin and camera table level.

The sleeping quarters all have private showers fresh-water heads with sinks, a queen size lower double, a commodious upper single and more drawers and hanging lockers than you ever dreamed of on a dive boat. The ships water maker produces 2000 gallons of fresh water per day, almost instantly hot in the showers. In the introductory briefing it isn't even suggested that the guests take sea-going showers. E-6 processing is performed three times a day and the videographer has a look at the tape from the last dive within minutes of drying off. A big wall-mounted video with a Hi8 deck reposes in the corner of the lounge. It all hangs out there, the good, the bad and the ugly shooting. A collection of Hollywood pot boilers, thrillers and classics Hollywood films fill in a library for evening entertainment.

The *Palau Aggressor II* is in direct competition with Peter Hughes *Sun Dancer*.

The *Sun Dancer* made a preview appearance at the DEMA (Dive Equipment Manufactures Association) convention in New Orleans in 1994. He docked that new and beautifully appointed boat right by the Aquarium and sent out several hundred invitations to a cocktail reception aboard. We all attended, invitations or not. I sneaked under the tent flap. Our eye balls popped out. There were linen table cloths and settings with crested porcelain and crystal wine glasses (at least they looked like crystal). The boutique was a little shop with a glass door and each cabin had its own head and shower with great commodious bunks. To cap it all, monogrammed bathrobes were invitingly hung on the closet doors of the staterooms. I am sure that if you anted up you could buy one at the end of the trip, just like in the great hotels. What ever, the bathrobes were a master stroke of showmanship. We learned that this floating pleasure dome was headed out into the western Pacific to compete with the *Palau Aggressor* on its own turf.

So, now, Palau has, what are probably the two finest Live-Aboard dive boats in the world, often moored at the dive sites within hailing distance of one another. Both are apotheosis of all that has been learned about Live-Aboards during their years of development. It fell out, over the years, that I would host tours with the Aggressor Fleet, as many as eight a year, so my judgment in comparing the Dancers with Aggressors is not entirely objective. But, this I can state with assurance: *Competition has engendered wonder-*

ful improvements. We divers have been the happy beneficiaries.

Please note: All this is hardly a comprehensive history of Live-Aboards. I haven't even touched on the fleet of Live-Aboards used by See & Sea Travel out of San Francisco, certainly the largest dive tour operator (wholesaler) in the U.S., if not the world. Run by Carl Roessler, a fine photographer and much published author in his own right, his company uses, at last count, sixteen different Live-Aboards that operate in exotic locations around the world. Many of the owners of these smaller Live-Aboard operations certainly have a vivid history worth telling, but this will have to be reserved for another publication.

Stan Waterman

Live-Aboard Advantages
over
Shore Based Diving

For serious diving with the comforts and convenience of an all inclusive resort, Live-Aboards provide the ultimate logistics. Being able to have your bed literally on top of a world class dive site and dive it at will, simply is a divers euphoria.

1) No more lugging dive gear. Quality Live-Aboards will provide you with a way to neatly stow your gear. This allows for you to organize your gear once and have it in the same place for the entire trip.

2) More diving freedom. Live-Aboards tend to allow a diver more freedom away from the group. You will see more marine life when diving with just one other person as opposed to 4-8 other divers.

3) Photography services. Most vessels have E-6 processing allowing for you to learn as you shoot. If you're shooting video, you can check and edit your results on the video monitor.

4) More comfort during surface intervals. Divers don't have to sit around in their wet suits on a crowded boat or a sandy beach with bugs. Instead, they can stretch out on the sundeck, read a book,

watch a video, or take a nap in your cool air conditioned state-room.

5) More dives each day. Four to five dives average are offered by most Live-Aboards.

6) No bugs. Get away from annoying sand fleas, mosquitoes and bugs which frequently reside in the tropics. Offshore anchorages on Live-Aboards are virtually bug free. This is especially important, in areas where malaria is a problem.

7) Better reefs. This is not always true, but overall, Live-Aboards frequent areas that day charter boats can't reach. Since marine life is sensitive to the presence of divers, the less impacted areas are usually a long way from easy land access.

8) More adventure. Live-Aboards, which venture in very remote areas, generally provide a more adventurous atmosphere, often emphasized by land excursions and unique cultural experiences.

9) Flexibility. In many remote destinations, Live-Aboard operators have the unique capability to keep their itinerary flexible. As mentioned in the *"Booking"* chapter, some agents tend to promise exact itineraries. When the weather conditions remain stable, the scheduled route may work out just fine, but when the weather turns, many Live-Aboards have the flexibility to change their route to hide from poor weather conditions.

Mothership Diving
And Advanced Skills

If the diving is done directly from the Live-Aboard vessel, the diving set up is referred to as *mothership diving*, as opposed to *tender diving* (see drift diving), which is usually practiced where strong currents are present, or if it's too deep to moor or anchor the larger vessel.

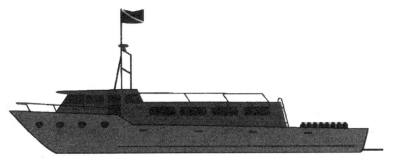

Assuming no strong currents frequent the area, diving directly from a large dive boat, while moored directly over the dive site, is definitely one of the major benefits of Live-Aboard diving. Here you will have plenty of opportunity to thoroughly explore pristine reefs. If you have an equipment failure or forget something, you can go straight back to the boat, fix the problem, and descend again, with minimum delay to yourself or your buddy. Generally these boats allow for two to three dives in each site. Since there's plenty of time, divers can stagger their entry time, thus eliminating underwater rush hour dive crowds.

You can expect to receive a thorough boat briefing once the entire group has arrive aboard. The captain, or on board manager, will inform you about emergency boat procedures, water conservation, meal schedules, house cleaning, bar rules and of course, dive deck procedures, rules and etiquette. The following is a basic **sample** of general procedures and scheduling many Live-Aboards practice.

A typical daily schedule is:

6:30 am - 8:00 am - Breakfast

8:00 am - Dive briefing. Dive deck open from 8:00-12:00.

Most divers hit the water by at least 8:30 am and dive for 30-60 minutes.

9:30 am - Surface interval. Snacks are usually provided to hold you over till lunch. You'll have time to sunbathe and plan the second dive based on what your first profile was like.

For photographers, videographers and enthusiastic underwater naturalists, this type of diving is ideal. Familiarity with the dive site and marine life, is a big key to great underwater photos, video and critter identification. Being able to dive the same site within hours of the first dive, gives photographers the opportunity to change camera formats if necessary. Or get a shot of that rare critter you found, after you ran out of film on the first dive.

11:00 - Enter the water for the second dive

12:00 - Lunch. Often the captain will move the vessel to a shallower reef where you will have an opportunity to do two afternoon dives and a night dive.

2:00 pm - First afternoon dive.

5:00 pm - Second afternoon dive.

6:00 pm - Dinner

8:30 pm - Night dive.

This is just a sample schedule that many Live-Aboards operate by. Of course not all divers make every dive, and diving at special times, such as dawn dives, can be arranged.

Dive site departure times are usually posted or announced. Please be sure to get back on board in time. If you return late it may force the captain to alter the planned schedule and dive site for the rest of that day. Generally not to the guests' benefit.

Dive Tips and Advanced Mothership Dive Skills

• **The dive deck** is one the most important features on a Live-Aboard, specially if mothership diving is practiced. If you dive 4-5 times a day, you will be spending more time here, than in your cabin. Most of the modern vessels' dive decks are spacious and feature individual lockers or baskets to store personal items such as flashlights, gloves, slates, booties, hoods, masks and other accessories. If you leave these small, but important items lying around, they can easily get lost, mixed up with other divers' equipment, blown off by the wind, washed off by a wave, etc. Because these storage areas generally get wet, but maybe the only "personal" storage area, it is a good idea to have a dry box (pelican box) for those items you need to keep dry.

• **Tanks** are usually conveniently located to make changing over to a full tank simple. Some boats have two per dive station. With this system you only need to unhook the regulator and BCD from the tank and slide it onto the full one at your station. Recently more boats are switching to "fill whips" so that they can fill the tank in place. This allows you to leave the BCD on the same tank during the whole trip. Both systems make handling equipment easy and hassle free.

Often the crew will do all the equipment set up for you. But, **always** double check: Did they actually do the change over? Since working the back deck can be a very busy job, it is not uncommon for a crew member to get distracted by other duties, thus unintentionally forgetting to do the tank switch for you.

Is the BCD in the right position? Some BCDs need to sit higher on the tanks than others in order to avoid the tank hitting you on the head while diving.

No matter how nice and efficient the crew is, **you** should take the ultimate responsibility for your equipment.

Tip: Never assume your new tank is full. Don't just turn your air on, always check your pressure gauge. At the same time, never assume, that, just because your gauge reads 3000 psi, that the air is actually turned **all** the way on. You, or someone else, may have turned it on, to check the tank pressure, but turned the valve off because your dive was delayed. Pressure will remain in the system, unless purged, making it appear as if the air is switched on. Or, the valve may be turned on only **half way**. If this is the case, your air supply may appear sufficient at the surface, or in shallow water, but as you gain depth, breathing will become harder and sporadic and your pressure gauge will fluctuate. You can resolve this problem by turning the valve on the rest of the way. **Or, you can avoid this problem by being sure to check the gauge and the tank valve, before entering the water on every dive**.

After you've inspected your equipment, slip into your BCD, often just by sitting in front of it and buckling up, then walk over to the entry area. On most vessels you should have your mask and fins in a position where you can easily reach them from the place of entry. If there are stairs leading down to the entry platform, walk down backwards, facing the ladders. Besides being safer, you will avoid banging your tank along the steps. Don't don your mask (unless you wear prescription lenses) and your fins, until you're at the waters edge and you are ready to enter.

The majority of the modern Live-Aboards have dive platforms that provide the diver with easy access in and out of the water. Preferably, the platform is large enough, for you and your buddy to don fins and masks and and a divemaster to assist you. Platforms that are within a few feet of the waterline make handling of accessory equipment safer and simpler. The use of the giant stride is generally the preferred entry technique. If you have a problem carrying your tank on your back, you can ask the crew to assist you with a seated entry, or, don it in the water.

Some motherships have exit points located on the side of the vessel. Usually these are higher off the water and make it more difficult to handle accessories. For divers without cameras, etc., this exit is often less congested and more convenient. Expect it to be higher off the water than the platform, thus requiring a farther drop into the water. Be sure to have a firm grip on your mask and weight belt as you enter.

Descents and Equalization

Some boat operations put out stern lines to hold the vessel over a particular spot, while others let the boat swing over the reef and/or wall. If you need a line to descend, either use the stern line, if available, or the "hang" or decompression line/bar, which usually descends 15-20 feet or more, off the vessel's stern. This method of descent can be of great assistance to a diver with "slow clearing ears." Many divers have ear trauma on descent that could be avoided if they used a descent line. A descent line keeps a diver from fighting shallow water buoyancy effects. If you make a steady progression down the line, no faster than your ears will clear, and avoid bouncing up and down, you will find ear clearing more efficient and successful.

If you are used to diving off day charter boats, utilizing the bow (anchor) line for you descent, do not attempt to surface swim to the anchor line of a 100 foot plus Live-Aboard. By the time you get to the bow line, you may already be too exhausted to make the dive. If you need to get to the anchor line, descend a few feet and swim along the keel of the vessel to the line. You will find that swimming under the surface to be far less exhausting.

Generally speaking, it is much more convenient to use a stern line. If for some reason there is no stern line available, explain to the crew that you have slow clearing ears and ask them to put a (weighted) line down.

Advanced Entry and Exit Skills

Presented here are skills, we have learned over the years and that are practiced routinely by professional and veteran divers. Make no mistake, these are truly **advanced** skills and should only be practiced within your own personal limitations and at your own risk. You must determine yourself, if you can safely perform these skills. In the following we describe each skill and provide precautionary measures and what to anticipate to avoid undue injury.

Entry:

We have found that the most efficient entry/descent technique to be a direct descent, as you enter the water.

Providing that your **ears equalize easily**, you don't **overweight** yourself drastically and your buddy is ready to also enter once you clear the entry point, try entering the water with no air in your BCD and continue to sink. You will need to begin equalizing immediately as you hit the water. **(Don't attempt this, if you overweight yourself. You'll sink like a rock, causing potentially major ear trauma, due to the inability to equalize quickly enough.)** If the divemaster is handing you a camera, turn around right after you hit the water, grasp the dive platform (*sea conditions permitting*) with one hand, receive your camera with the other, **then**, continue to sink.

Next, make sure you clear the entry area immediately so that your buddy doesn't jump on top of you. You can then wait in shallow water, 10 feet or so, for your buddy.

Most divers find this far more comfortable, than bobbing at the surface while waiting for their partner. *(You can use the time to adjust camera arms, slip on your gloves, double check that you have a full tank and your computer is activated.)* If you do choose this technique, remember to inform your buddy, when making a dive plan. Otherwise your buddy may very possibly assume you already left, thus worrying about you and/or choosing to buddy up with someone else.

Gentle Entry

This entry is for situations where unusual marine life encounters are present close by the boat. Often, we have observed that, if the divemaster draws everybody's attention with: "Manta Ray/Turtle/Whaleshark/Dolphins, right underneath/next to the boat," everybody just races to the dive platform with or without tank, giant strides into the water with a giant "splash," and before you even have a chance to look around, the animal(s) have been spooked away. Check with the dive master for suggestions, but we recommend, that you (carefully) walk down the ladder backwards into the water, with all gear in place, except fins, including regulator/snorkel in your mouth, then, *slip* on your fins at the bottom of the ladder and **gently** slide into the water. Chances are the animal of attraction may stick around.

The main point being, marine life is very sensitive to water disturbances such as divers jumping into the water. You will greatly increase you chance of a positive encounter if you cautiously enter the water and slowly approach the animal.

Exiting in Rough Water Conditions

Exiting the water creates a transition factor that often places the diver into an awkward and sometimes dangerous situation. Upon exiting, a diver goes from near weightlessness, to full body weight, plus at least an extra 50-60 pounds of dive equipment. Welcome back to gravity!!! This is one of the "clumsiest" positions for many divers. Add rough water and turbid ocean conditions, along with a bouncing 80-100 foot dive boat and the difficulty factor is greatly increased. In this situation we have found the following technique to be very effective for many divers.

For vessels which have deep ladders (3-4 feet plus), which allow a diver to stay underwater while removing their fins, this technique allows for a quick and balanced exit:

1) When approaching the mothership to exit, swim toward the **bottom** of the ladder, with your arm outstretched, making sure you keep your head clear of the ladders. Be alert. In rough conditions, ladders may be slamming up and down, often generating a swirl of white water around them, thus, making the ladder difficult to see.

2) Once you reach the bottom of the ladder, take a firm, but flexible grip on the bottom step or bar. Utilize the elbow joint as your shock absorber to avoid shoulder injuries and to absorb the movement of the ladder. Your body weight should slow down the slamming.

WARNING: Never remove your fins until you have a firm but flexible grip on the ladder. Many times we have seen divers float away from the boat, out of control, due to no fins. Do not hold on to the ladders at the top end if water conditions are rough. It's like riding a bucking bull and possibly as dangerous.

3) Remove your fins **while submerged**. Slide your fin straps over your wrists as you remove them, or if you're wearing full foot fins, slide them under your armpit. This will keep your hands free for balance and a hand hold, as you walk quickly out of the water, with all other gear in place, **including your mask and regulator**.

Many divers feel it's easier to hand your fins to the divemaster, which may be true, if he's available. But this "need" for assistance can create real problems if the time arises when the divemaster may be assisting another diver, or not be available for you at the very second you were counting on him.

Veteran divers learn to develop self reliance so that when the situation dictates it, they have a solid plan and the skills to safely deal with the ever changing environment the ocean provides.

Yes, it's true that on most Live-Aboards the divemaster is there on the platform to take your fins and other accessories **most** of the time, but what if they aren't? Isn't it YOUR responsibility to develop the proper skills to take care of yourself??? You can always throw your fins up on the platform, but in rough water you run a high risk that the next wave will sweep them back into the ocean.

We **HIGHLY** recommend you practice this exit technique in calm seas before attempting it in rough water. In fact, for those of you who just get into the habit of exiting this way all the time, you will thank yourself later, when the water gets rougher. This is the technique we teach our students to use in all conditions. With practice you should be able to do a dive without having to spend **any time** on the surface.

If you're a photographer or videographer and need to hand up a camera, surface **out of the range of the slamming ladders,** just enough to get your eyes above the waterline. Don't inflate your BCD, that just makes you bulky and less streamlined. Get the divemaster's attention, **then**, approach the dive platform quickly, making sure you stay away from the ladders. Hand up your camera and descend again and follow the steps described above.

If, for some reason, you're unable to exit with this method-for example, you are unable to remove your fins without help and you must come to the surface to get assistance-leave your mask on your face and your regulator in your mouth until you are standing on the dive platform. If you were to fall back in, you would at least have **air** and be able to **see** what's happening.

Another possible rough water exit technique is a deep water exit, which involves handing up the weight belt, then the **inflated** BCD with tank, followed by crawling up the ladders quickly. If you must resort to this technique, again, leave your mask and fins on and **utilize your snorkel for airway control**.

As with all diving activities, there may also be some other options based on the vessel configuration and actual degree of turbid water and currents presently affecting the situation. Your crew will advise.

Navigation

Although possible when requested, Live-Aboard diving usually does not include following a divemaster on every dive. As a rule, you and your buddy are "on your own." This certainly has many advantages. You can swim at your own pace, look for critters you're interested in and avoid underwater crowds. With this freedom comes the responsibility of developing underwater navigational skills. An introduction to basic navigation skills can be learned in an advanced open water course and/or underwater navigation specialty course.

Though the compass is a valuable piece of diving equipment, many divers are under the impression that it is an automatic underwater boat finder. Unfortunately, this is not the case. Veteran divers rely mostly on natural navigation while diving in tropical oceans. They utilize a great variety of natural references to determine their location relative to the exit point.

For destinations where you are diving along a wall, navigation is usually a simple out and back pattern along the wall with your main concern being depth control. But when diving flat reefs with only gradual sloping, navigation skills become an important concern. Since there are several good books on the subject and a variety of options to learning underwater navigation skills, we will not attempt to duplicate that process in this publication. It is important to point out that, you will greatly enhance your safety and enjoyment with competent underwater navigational skills, when diving from a Live-Aboard.

Tip: If you're still inexperienced with navigation, remember, some of the most interesting marine life is often very close to, or directly under the boat. If you're in any doubt at all of your whereabouts, make sure you begin to get your bearings with at least 1500 psi left in your tank. When absolutely necessary, surface. If your dive was deep and circumstances permit, do a safety stop, before you surface.

Make sure, you and your buddy agree on the signal "Where is the boat." While you may worry the whole dive, how to find your way back, your buddy may know exactly where to go. If you see a crew member, ask them where the boat is. (With many operations crew members use a different color tank, and are easily recognizable).

You will find that generally, mothership diving to be the easiest form of recreational diving available today. If you are new to Live-Aboards, we recommend you begin your Live-Aboard diving from one of these vessels.

Drift Diving

Drift, or live boat diving, is defined as entering the water in one location and being picked up by the boat wherever you surface. Practiced in locations that won't allow for anchoring a large vessel or, where the currents are so strong, divers wouldn't be able to return to the mothership. The diving is done from launches, averaging about 18 - 22 ft., designed of  either rubber (inflatables), fiberglass or aluminum. All are functional and generally adequate for the logistics involved in diving a particular destination.

Sometimes drift diving is practiced directly from the mothership. If currents, wind, shallow reefs and/or swells are present, pickups and drop offs, can be quite tricky and put both, divers and the mothership, in potentially dangerous situations.

Under these conditions, there is very little margin for error. If the wind pushes the ship toward the reef while a diver is struggling with his fins at the exit ladders, which are generally located near the propellers, the captain has placed himself into a no win situation. We tend to avoid mothership drift diving unless the conditions allow for it safely.

True drift dives take place in locations where currents are present, often in channel openings or outer offshore pinnacles. Since there is a significant flow of nutrient rich water, you will generally find an explosion of marine life. Here is where you are most likely to encounter large pelagics. You will also notice most of the reef fish up off the reef, feeding in the current.

Logistics involved:

1) you begin the dive by entering the water at a specific point,

2) ride the current along a wall or reef structure,

3) surface, when you are low on air, and

4) wait for the launch to pick you up.

Sounds easy ... right?

The fact is, drift diving is considered advanced diving due to the personal demands required of each diver.

When diving in a strong current a diver must be able to:

1) descend without a line, and equalize the ears quickly,

2) manage various degrees of currents, which can include up or down currents,

3) maintain buddy contact, and

4) perform a safety stop without a line to control buoyancy.

True drift diving needs to be approached with a solid plan!

When being transported to the dive site by skiff, some operations require you to ride with your BCD, tank and weight belt donned, while others have you don the gear once you get close. If the site has little to no current, the procedures become much more relaxed, but if a strong to moderate current is present, possibly with a strong wind blowing, it becomes crucial, that you act quickly, but deliberately, when the divemaster or skiff driver gives instructions.

When the driver tells you to get ready, put your fins and mask on, along with the rest of your gear.

If you must wear gloves, make sure you have those on, or better, carry them in your BCD pocket, and put them on, once under water.

If you wait too long to gear up, you could miss the entry point and get blown off the dive site in a moderate to heavy current. Often the boat driver can reposition the boat for your entry, but if your buddy has already entered and descended, it may be difficult or impossible to reunite. Also, keep in mind the driver can not maneuver the boat, if there is a diver in the water near the props of the boat.

Entering the water:

Generally the preferred method of entry is the back roll.

We suggest that you enter the water with very little or no air in your BCD. If the current is running, it's important for you to be able to descend as quickly as possible, without having to fiddle with trapped air in your BCD. As mentioned in the *"Mothership Diving - Advanced skills,"* you must be able to equalize you ears easily and not overweight yourself, if you enter the water with no air in your BCD.

Sit on the edge of the launch, facing into the boat. **Be sure that all your accessories are clear so as not to get hung up on the boat as you enter.** Fold hoses and gauges over your lap, clip them securely to your BCD or keep them in your BCD pocket, if that is possible.

With a glance over your shoulder, or by asking the divemaster or launch driver, check that the entry area behind you is clear.

Place one hand on your mask, keep your regulator in your mouth, and with all gear clear, just let the weight of the tank take you backwards.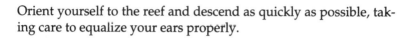

If you have a camera, let the divemaster hand it to you upon surfacing.

Orient yourself to the reef and descend as quickly as possible, taking care to equalize your ears properly.

Get to depth, or close to the bottom as quickly as you can. Currents are weaker and generally more manageable closer to the wall and/or bottom. At this point you can just drift or you may get behind a rock or a ledge, just out of the current, where you often find a vast variety of life in the current swept water column above your head. This is an excellent way to observe sharks, tuna, jacks and barracuda. When you want to move on, just get back in the current and drift.

Follow your dive plan and make sure you include a safety stop at the end of the dive. Keep in mind, if you are, at any time, swimming **into** the current you will use a lot more air than expected!

When diving in strong currents, it is common for divers to find themselves off the main reef and in blue water (water too deep to see any bottom or reef references). These circumstances make recommended safety stops more difficult. If you stay within visual reference of the reef, you simplify navigating and performing safety stops. It will also be easier for the tender driver to find you, minimizing uncomfortable time waiting at the surface.

To enter the water in areas with little to no current, you may find, that by placing your equipment with the BCD partially inflated, into the water and don it in the water works well for you. For divers with a bad back, this method is a viable alternative. Practice this technique in calm water before attempting it in rough turbulent conditions.

Exiting the water:

End the dive by swimming away from the reef into deeper water, then surface. This will allow the tender driver some space to maneuver and the time to get you out of the water before the boat drifts onto the reef.

When approaching the launch, make sure the driver is not maneuvering, and gives you the "ok" to approach.

Hand up your camera or dive light to the divemaster, followed by your weight belt, and **then** your scuba unit.

Some operations will have you walk up a ladder with your gear on, while others will have you take the BCD off in the water and they will pull it up for you.

If you choose to board the boat by kicking over the side, leave your fins on to help you kick yourself onto the boat.

If you are using the ladder, leave your fins on until you are actually holding onto the ladder. There may be a current, and if you take off your fins and mask to early, you may have a hard time catching up with the boat.

An example of drift diving conditions:

Cocos Island / Costa Rica.

The mothership is anchored and tenders transport you to the dive site. Strong currents are the usual. In fact the stronger the current, the better the chances of seeing sharks and other pelagics.

Due to the rigorous conditions, this location is not suitable for beginners. Cocos receives 25 feet of rain annually, so many days are rainy and/or overcast. This makes finding divers on the surface difficult. For safety purposes it's a good idea not to get caught in the currents that will take you off the dive sites, into blue water. You may easily be carried off for miles.

This is a classic example of a destination where you should carry signaling devices and brightly colored equipment at all times. The tenders will pick you up wherever you surface as long as they can ... see you.

The use of cameras can complicate all of this, especially if you are not a seasoned diver. Don't start your underwater photo career here.

Current Diving

Since currents are usually associated with tidal movement, they are generally more apparent at the surface than in deeper water. Often you can escape a current, by simply descending into greater depths. However, the key to dealing with currents is, to hide from them or go with them. Ebb currents, close to the edge of the wall, can create currents perpendicular to the wall, pushing you up or down the wall. Sometimes you can encounter "whirlpools," where up and down currents combine like in a blender. You can attempt to descend a little, but it really

works best, "if you hug the wall." Move within a foot along the wall, taking advantage of every outcropping you can tuck behind, until you find the strength of the current subsiding, which is often the case after only a few yards.

Generally, avoid swimming unnecessarily into the current. Go with the flow, whenever appropriate. But at times, if you want to observe shark action, or to make your way to the dive site, you might have to swim up current. If this is the case, move as close to the bottom or wall, as possible. It can be helpful, if you pull yourself along, taking a handhold on rocks. This requires a lot less energy than kicking, which equates to less air usage on your part.

Please, *do not grab the coral! Coral is far too fragile to withstand the pressure of you pulling yourself into a strong current. You can easily break off whole coral structures, damaging the reef severely.*

If you carry a bulky camera, probably with long strobe arms, and heavy strobes, moving into the current becomes literally an even greater "drag." Fold the arms, and streamline your camera apparatus as much as possible. Once you're out of the current, or found a protected little niche, where you can rest and observe marine life, you can reset your strobe arms.

Safety Equipment Recommendations

Most operations that utilize tenders to perform drift dives on a regular basis, are good at spotting the divers on the surface. But, for your own comfort and safety, we'd like to suggest the following special equipment considerations for drift diving.

Even though we haven't received a federal grant to study the theory that **bright colors** are easier to spot in a turbulent sea than **dark colors**, we feel pretty confident that **bright orange** is the easiest color to see on the surface of the ocean. This is widely supported by the fact that the Coast Guard requires all safety devices to be colored orange. You will also find evidence of high visibility in the fact that all road crews also wear this bright color. Unfortunately at this time, since the consumer deemed the color unpopular, no SCUBA manufactures produce an orange BCD anymore. Other high visibility colors such as hot pink, and lime green, can also be seen well in the ocean environment. Although fluorescent yellow and white may look like a bright color in the dive shop, and possibly even underwater, at the surface of a turbulent, choppy sea with white caps, you'd be surprised how difficult they are to spot.

By far the most difficult colors to see are **blue, black and green (teal)**.

*I know, I know ... someone told you sharks like the colors orange and red **better**, than blue and black. Well, the way I got it figured is, if I'm not on the surface for a long time, sharks are not an issue. Also, aren't sealions, the favorite food of Great White sharks, black/brown ?*

When looking for divers at the surface, what the tender driver sees first is, what is **above** the surface. The color of your knee pads, or even of the bottom of your BCD is negligible.

Divers with brightly colored wet suit shoulders and sleeves along with brightly colored upper half of their BCD, and hood, if they wear one, are much easier to locate.

Your fins are also important. If necessary you can take one fin off, and waive it over your head, increasing your visibility considerably.

We have even met divers who placed **flares** into flashlight cases. That's right, **signal flares** for lost ships. Even though airlines strictly forbid the transportation of these items, a diver's fear of being lost at sea, can overcome any common sense.

We don't go as far as recommending you carry an arsenal of flares, (Even Skyblazer's new Emergency and Locating Flares for divers, are illegal on planes) but we do believe you can increase your chances of being spotted quickly on the surface in **all** conditions by considering the colors of your basic equipment, and with the following diver safety signaling devices:

"Sausages" are orally inflatable signaling devices, available in several bright colors, of which, of course the preferred color is **orange**. With only a few puffs of air these devices can be inflated to a length of 3 - 6 feet, depending on the manufacturer. When deflated, they can be rolled into a tight package and easily carried in your BCD pocket.

"Signal Mirrors" (Skyblazer) can easily be carried in your BCD pocket, and can be used as a locating device at the surface. These specially designed mirrors are supposed to be visible for up to ten miles, even on hazy, overcast days.

Chemical Light sticks are recommended for night diving. If you're planning to use the product solely for emergency use, they can be carried in your BCD pocket or clipped to your BCD. Once activated most light sticks last for approximately six hours. These devices are cheap, but can only be used once. There are several new products out, which generate the same light effect as light sticks, but are designed for multiple use. These products are considerably more expensive and often require batteries (Something else to check on). If you're planning to use the product solely for emergency use, we recommend chemical light sticks. (During night drift dives, at least one **back up flashlight** is a must! Make sure your secondary light is actually working. If you carry it in your BCD pocket, chances are, that it got left on and the batteries are already exhausted. If you're on a drift dive at night with no light source, your chances of being spotted are **slim**!)

Commonly used Noise Devices:

Dive Alert. Blows a loud high pitched squeal, that can be heard for a long distance. This device works off the air pressure of your tank and is easy to install.

Specially recommended for night dives, and during rain squalls, when colors are almost moot.

Storm Whistle. This is a specially designed whistle that can be heard from far away. Manual operation, no tank air pressure required.

Note: The distance these noise devices can be heard from is of course **very** dependent on the direction the wind is blowing!!!

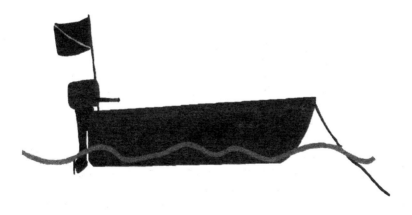

Buddy System

You learned it in your open water class: SCUBA diving is safest if performed as a buddy team.

One of the nice things about diving off Live-Aboards is, that even if you don't arrive with a buddy you can always buddy up, without being "herded into a group," like many day charters attempt to do.

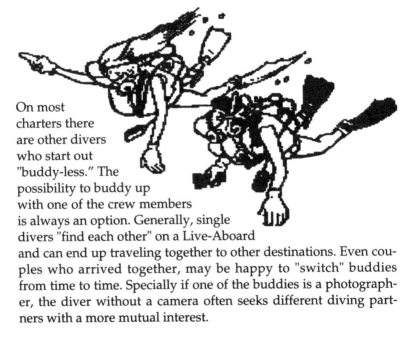

On most charters there are other divers who start out "buddy-less." The possibility to buddy up with one of the crew members is always an option. Generally, single divers "find each other" on a Live-Aboard and can end up traveling together to other destinations. Even couples who arrived together, may be happy to "switch" buddies from time to time. Specially if one of the buddies is a photographer, the diver without a camera often seeks different diving partners with a more mutual interest.

As a beginner, you should seek as much education as possible and dive in destinations which fit your experience level. The more comfortable you are, the more you will enjoy your dive. Diving with a buddy is usually safer and more fun since you share your experiences and can point out marine life to each other. Overall you should try to find a buddy with approximately the same experience level.

Apply the basic dive planning skills you learned in your SCUBA course such as:

1) Discussing time and depth limits
2) Deciding who will navigate
3) Agreeing on what to do if currents, unique marine life sightings or other unexpected factors cause you to alter your plan.
4) Discussing emergency procedures.

In addition, compare each others skill level, equipment configurations and hand signals. If you put aside a few minutes before every dive for planning, you probably will eliminate any potential frustration and misunderstandings underwater, thus making your experience much more enjoyable and safe.

Photography and Solo Diving

There are divers, especially experienced photographers, who don't want to buddy up. Buddy diving can be a "handicap" to the U/W photographer who is trying to get a quality photo of a skittish critter. The presence of another diver often makes marine life harder to approach. But, unfortunately, due to liability, American owned dive boats must be strict on the rules of the buddy system. Divers who want to dive solo, pose a liability problem for the operation. Divers should understand, that often, when a crew member imposes the "buddy rule," it is only because the **insurance** companies set the rules. Most captains and crew members hate having to burden anybody with rules on their vacation, but in a court of law, they must be able to defend everything that they did and didn't do. If a crew member knowingly allows a diver to dive alone and an accident occurs, it is very likely everyone associated with the boat and the operation will be named in a lawsuit, even if the diver demanded to dive alone to start with.

So, as you can see, the crew is usually just defending themselves and the operation. As a captain, I have always found it to be unpleasant having to reprimand adults for breaking the rules, but going to court is worse.

Professional Divers verses Recreational Sport Divers

People who are certified as Divemasters or SCUBA Instructors have proven a higher degree of education and responsibility in the SCUBA profession, at least in regards to insurance policies. They are insurable (liability) and qualified to teach others about the sport. It can be assumed that they understand the risk involved in solo diving. For this reason, even US owned vessel operators, sometimes make exceptions and permit professional divers to dive solo.

How dangerous is solo diving?

That is a question every diver should think about. Since conditions and diver skill level vary widely, it is impossible to answer that question with a generalization. One theory is that a diver, who knows he is diving solo, will act more cautious and conservative to start with. Diving with a buddy can possibly give a false sense of security. If you are an experienced diver and are buddied up with a beginner, you probably end up "taking care" of your buddy. Perhaps you want to do so, but you probably realize that, in the event that you experience an emergency, your buddy may not be competent enough to really assist you. They often just become a witness to the event. Instructors who dive with beginner students, or introductory divers, are a good example of this.

We do not condone solo diving and firmly believe that a competent, knowledgeable buddy team is a much safer and enjoyable way for most to dive. But, we also realize the fact that in many foreign countries, the Live-Aboards who have no USA ownership, will often allow competent, experienced divers to dive in a "loose" buddy system or alone. Since it is virtually impossible to sue them, they take a more "be responsible for your own actions" approach. Personally we find this approach refreshing and usually quite appealing to the experienced Diver/Underwater photographer.

So in reality, the choice often is your own, with the bottom line being, if you do choose to dive alone, you better be prepared with experience, knowledge and equipment. There are books on the subject of solo diving and we suggest you read them.

Dive Equipment Considerations

Since confidence and safety come with familiarization with ones equipment, we highly recommend for you to bring your own equipment. Live-Aboards usually only have a limited supply of rental equipment, if available at all. And, although there may be exceptions, the rental gear is mostly of inferior quality, generally neglected and poorly maintained.

If you do plan to rent equipment from the boat, make sure you communicate that to the vessel. Contact the vessel's office or your booking agent, or even better, both. It's amazing how many messages don't get passed on!

You may want to rent equipment from your local dive shop, if you don't have your own gear. You can thoroughly inspect your equipment and make sure it fits right.

Purchasing "travel friendly" equipment

Diving is an equipment intensive sport, and it's important that you purchase reliable quality gear. If you plan to travel out of the USA and beyond the Caribbean and Bahamas, buy name brand equipment. Few SCUBA manufactures have a true world wide presence. If you have a hose blow that is a special size, it is less-likely that it can be replaced in many remote destinations without special adapters, that are not always readily available. In fact, it's unlikely that you'll even find someone qualified to repair most equipment brands, let alone stocked with the proper parts.

When presented with equipment problems, veteran divers have discovered the value of brand name equipment and their parts availability. What one saves in dollars in the dive shop, may cost him in inconvenience and disappointment somewhere in New Guinea.

Tip: Beware of equipment with new and unique features unless you can carry all the "special parts" as back up and know how to work on it yourself.

Specific Gear Considerations

For information on color and its safety purposes see the Equipment section of *Drift Diving*.

• Mask

Before you embark for your Live-Aboard adventure, check your mask. The skirt may have become brittle, cracked, or deformed and may leak. Also, it's always a possibility, that, during your trip someone steps on your mask, a tanks falls on it, you drop it into 1000 feet of water, etc. Consider a second mask as a back up.

• Snorkel

Snorkels and SCUBA diving are kind of like spare tires and cars, they are only valuable when needed. In your open water class you learn to always have a snorkel attached to your mask strap, mainly for safety purposes. The reason : to simplify breathing while on the surface. Well, for the most part, divers seldom spend much time on the surface when diving from a boat. So, why should boat divers wear snorkels? Answer: If you run low on air and have to swim back to the boat on the surface.

Often you'll find veteran divers who never carry a snorkel. Of course as long as they watch their air supply and have excellent navigation skills, a snorkel goes unused. But, if one is to get lost or pulled out to sea and left drifting for hours, a snorkel may keep a diver alive. Now, there are times when a snorkel can become a hindrance while wreck diving or penetrating into other tight areas, such as caves, overhangs, tunnels, etc. Still, you should take a snorkel with you on your dive whether you wear it on your mask strap, or keep it in your pocket. This way it is available if you need it. (Another good reason to keep a snorkel handy, is for that moment when a pod of dolphins swims close to the boat and you get a rare opportunity to swim with them, on snorkel.)

• **Dive Computers**

Dive Computers are a **must** on a Live-Aboard. If you really want to get the most out of your trip then invest in a dive computer. Diving from the tables is generally inefficient and unpractical. A quality computer, if used properly, enhances your safety and enjoyment. Dive computers give you the flexibility to do multi-level dives without the rigid guidelines imposed by other nitrogen measuring tables. They have proven the test of time and are a standard piece of equipment for almost all Live-Aboard veterans.

Diving with a computer requires you understand the symbols and numbers the computer is presenting. Don't wait till you're 85 feet deep to find out what it means to have a "ceiling" symbol come up on the computers screen. Read the manual **before** all else fails!!!

When computer diving keep in mind the basic concept that you never dive to the computers' limits, just as you should never dive to the limits of any dive table. You should also perform the deepest part of each dive toward the beginning, gradually working your way shallower and **always** perform **safety stops** at the end of **every dive**. One other consideration is that Live-Aboards allow divers to do multi-level dives over multiple days, this intern lends itself to continuous nitrogen saturation. One practice that some medical experts tout is for divers to sit out a few dives toward the middle of the week to allow for nitrogen off gassing.

New innovative dive computers

The market is loaded with quality dive computers. Be aware that the newest and highest tech computer, is not necessarily the most reliable one. It's always best to purchase a model that has proven the test of time. If you do want to have the newest "toy" on the market, be prepared for failure. So far, most new versions of dive computers have had "bugs" in the system when they first came out. It usually takes anywhere from 6 months to sometimes never, before "new innovative" versions of the dive computer work out their kinks.

Since these dive computers are constantly advancing, keeping up on the latest detailed features and modifications is beyond the scope of this guide. We suggest you do some careful research and look for a model that has a proven track record and is easy for you to read and understand. Check around, you will find some books and magazine articles dedicated to the specifications of each dive computer model.

• Back up Computers

With the price of some quality dive computers now under $300, most divers **can't** afford **not** to have a **backup dive computer**. If you have a computer malfunction, or simply forget to turn on your computer (There are still many models you have to manually activate) or the battery fails between dives, most computer manuals suggest, that you wait **24 hours** before you dive again.

Now, we can't tell you how many times we have seen a diver's computer fail on their second dive of the day, or their third day of diving, while the boat is sitting on a beautiful pristine reef with unlimited visibility. This diver, who paid $300 a day for diving on a Live-Aboard, will inevitably, out of frustration, ask the crew when it will **really** be safe for him to dive?

Of course there is one simple answer: **In 24 hours!**

Unless, of course, the diver has a back up computer, **which he has taken on all the previous dives.** If you leave your back up computer on the boat in its case until your primary computer fails, you still have to wait 24 hours, because your back up computer has no way of tracking your present nitrogen level.

• Wet Suits

If the water is warm enough to dive without a wet suit, or a "shorty," we recommend you still wear a full body cover (lycra suit) to protect you from coral scratches and stinging plankton or jellyfish. For details on neoprene thickness, see "water temperatures" of *Choosing the right destination.*

• Buoyancy Control Device (BCD)

Choose a bright color *(see Drift Diving)* and become very familiar with its operation. Know where the air release valves are and the proper body position required to get the air out efficiently. Low volume BCDs should only be used by divers who require little to no weight to sink. These BCDs have very little lift and are inefficient for moderate to heavily weighted divers. A properly fitting BCD should be streamlined and not slide around on you.

Look for a BCD that will allow you to tuck in your gauges and hook off accessories to avoid damage to your equipment, as well as the reef. Generally, the fewer buckles and gadgets on the BCD, the fewer possibilities of breakage.

• Regulator

Some tropical locations feature swift currents and deep drop-offs. An easy breathing, well functioning regulator is important. In this category you usually get what you pay for. Comparing brands and models of a regulator while standing in a dive store where there is no current or surge affecting you, isn't an objective test. How a regulator breathes at depth under normal diving circumstances is the best way to truly compare brands and models. The very best way to test the true performance of a regulator, is to dive with it at **depth**. But, since this is not always practical, you can often check the breathing resistance of a regulator, utilizing a magna-helic meter. This meter is specifically designed to measure inhalation effort required and exhalation resistance of a system. The easiest way to get these specifications is usually from the dive equipment manufacturers advertisement of the specific unit you are interested in.

Service your regulator before each trip or annually.

Since proper breathing technique is an important key to being comfortable in the water, your air delivery system is a vital component.

If you own a regulator, have it overhauled before your trip or at least once a year. When picking your regulator up at the dive shop, test it on a tank and check how it breaths. If the shop has a magna-helic meter you can check it, using the meter. Make sure your alternate air source is also hooked up and the tank pressure is close to 3000 psi.

Leave it hooked to the tank with the air on for several minutes. If the intermediate pressure is too high, it will often take a couple of minutes for the pressure to "creep" up causing an annoying free flow. For many years we have witnessed recently overhauled regulators free flow on the first day of diving, due to poor tuning or lack of quality service.

• Alternate Air Source

We recommend an alternate air source such as the SCUBAPRO Air II, which eliminates a lot of problems caused by a dragging octopus. Because this alternate air source style doubles as your low pressure inflator, you'll be constantly using it, thus becoming familiar with its location very quickly. In an out-of-air emergency, this may be critical. Whatever configuration you dive with, make sure that it is functioning properly, not dragging across the reef and your buddy knows its location and function.

• Gloves

Divers wearing gloves are more likely to damage the reef. By touching marine life, such as octopi and nudibranchs with a gloved hand, you can damage the protective film layer which covers them, subjecting them to infections. Also you are a lot more likely to grab hold of delicate corals. Your goal should be to control your buoyancy in a way, that holding on to the reef becomes unnecessary. In some destinations they now prohibit gloves, to keep the divers from touching everything.

If you don't want to leave your gloves behind, try the option of carrying them in your BCD pocket. During your dive, if you feel like it becomes necessary to wear them, you can slip them on quickly. We have encountered stinging plankton while hanging out on our safety stops on buoy lines. Putting gloves on, kept the plankton from stinging our wrists and hands.

• Dive Knife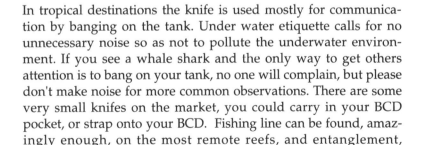

In tropical destinations the knife is used mostly for communication by banging on the tank. Under water etiquette calls for no unnecessary noise so as not to pollute the underwater environment. If you see a whale shark and the only way to get others attention is to bang on your tank, no one will complain, but please don't make noise for more common observations. There are some very small knifes on the market, you could carry in your BCD pocket, or strap onto your BCD. Fishing line can be found, amazingly enough, on the most remote reefs, and entanglement, although not likely, is possible.

In recent years more and more divers have gone to "tank bangers," which take the place of a knife for underwater noise making. These devices are usually made out of rubber and have a hard fiberglass ball that bangs on the tank when you pull it.

• Dive Lights

We recommend a smaller dive light for day diving. Preferably one you can keep in your BCD pocket and pull out when ever you want to explore a cave or crevice, or would just like to check out the true color of fish or a critter.

For night dives however, keep your small light in your pocket as a back up and use a large bright light as a primary. You can use rechargeable batteries if you like since most Live-Aboards have charging outlets.

Carry spare bulbs and o-rings for your flashlight. With some lights, you may even carry a spare switch and lens.

• Spare Parts and Tools

When ever possible, bring spare parts! Even if certain replacement parts are available in a resort or dive shop at a destination, it doesn't mean they are stocked up on the Live-Aboard itself. Since the right spare part can make the difference between a perfect dive vacation or one you had to miss dives because of equipment failure and/or worry about your equipment, you should pack at least the basics.

Never assume that tools are available on a Live-Aboard. Sometimes they are and often they are not. Or, they are the personal possession of one of the crew members, who tend to treat their tools like gold, and stow it under their bed, to prevent their tools to grow legs and go "walk about." Tools are very hard to come by, if you permanently reside on a boat, and crew members may be very reluctant, understandingly so, to lend out their tools.

Take your own, and you won't be at the mercy of others. In fact, you may end up the hero by helping out other divers.

41

We recommend the following tools:

- two crescent wrenches
- assorted screw drivers (flat heads and Phillips). Photographers may want to take along a set of jewelers screw drivers.
- hex or Allen wrenches or, A tool known as a "divers tool" has all of these in one. Check your local dive shop for availability.
- O-ring pick
- pliers

Spare parts should include:

- high and low pressure hoses
- o-rings for flashlights, tanks, regulator, photo equipment, etc.
- mask and fin straps
- extra flashlight bulbs
- regulator mouthpiece
- cable ties
- a back up regulator is a functional luxury to consider

These are some of the basic parts and tools that can save a dive for you. The amount of spares and specialty tools you carry with you is often based on your knowledge of equipment repair. **Never attempt to dismantle dive equipment you are not thoroughly familiar with.**

Reef Conservation and Marine Life

Since Live-Aboards often visit remote pristine reefs, it is your responsibility to treat the reefs accordingly. Try to think of the underwater world as an art gallery with innumerous fragile pieces. Diving from Live-Aboards offers untouched diving. Which often means unspoiled marine life. It is essential you understand that **you can make a difference.**

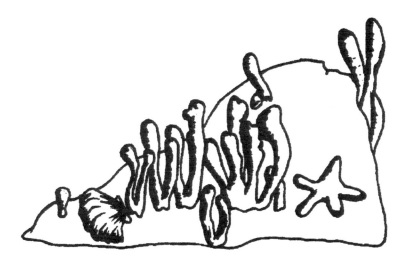

Divers, especially photographers and night divers, often do unforgivable damage to the reef. Many times, we have observed divers who are preoccupied photographing a small shrimp, but don't realize that their fins are wiping out all the surrounding coral. Activities, such as underwater photography can become a real challenge when currents and/or surge are pulling and pushing on you. When conditions are such, that you must hold on to the coral, or "plant" yourself on the reef in order to get the photo, it may be better to just enjoy the ride and keep your film for the next dive!

Night divers also present a potential hazard for the reef and its residents. Visually handicapped, due to low light, most divers "hug the reef" in the attempt to gain orientation, which often leads to accidental contact with the fragile coral and delicate seafans. Add a current to your night dive, and you may soon feel like an elephant in a china store when you are being shoved into a beautiful soft coral tree, before you're even able to see it! The diver may survive the "the dark of the night" underwater, but the reef inhabitants may not!!!

Perfect buoyancy skills are the key to **controlled** movement underwater. Divers need to **properly** weight themselves. Diving overweighted is not only harder on you, but can be catastrophic to the reef. Divers who are overweighted, kick with their fins pointed down, toward the reef. Fin damage is the **number one** offender to coral damage. Learn how to master your buoyancy, before you attempt underwater photography or other advanced dive specialties. Explore the potential to alter your buoyancy with controlled breathing. Once you've established neutral buoyancy, you can easily adjust your position by **anticipating** your path in, over and around the underwater terrain. For example, if you're approaching a pinnacle, or a colony of seafans, you can often raise yourself up and graciously float **over** the obstacle with a deliberate inhalation.

If you are negatively buoyant, you will find yourself sinking onto the reef when you stop to observe reef inhabitants. If you do find yourself crashing into the coral, look for a spot with no coral and push yourself off with **one** finger. Inhale. **Then**, adjust your BCD.

There are no perfect formulas for proper weighting for everyone in all diving conditions. What we have found works best for most divers, is to check your buoyancy at the **end** of the dive, assuming you are using an aluminum tank.

This should be done while you are performing a safety stop at approximately fifteen to twenty feet, and your tank is low on air (less than 800 psi). This is performed by removing **all** the air from the BCD. You then should be able to maintain neutral buoyancy through proper breathing technique and body position. If you start to sink, shed some weight before your next dive. If unable to safely perform a safety stop, due to positive buoyancy, add some weight.

The reason why you should wait till the end of the dive to fine tune your weighting is that aluminum tanks become buoyant at the end of the dive when most of the air is exhausted. Divers often describe this buoyant feeling as "having a cork on their back." With steel tanks this is less of a problem.

Another important "reef saving" practice is, to tuck away all dangling gear. Octopus regulators and gauges need to be secured to the diver, to prevent them from dragging across the reef. It is essential that divers place accessories such as flashlights, slates, and any other equipment away to prevent damage to the marine environment.

Remember, almost everything in the underwater world is alive! Stony corals may look like stones, but are actually colonies of tiny animals that form a calcareous skeleton around them. These tiny animals make up the foundation of our tropical reefs which takes thousands of years of growth to develop. We, as scuba divers, must take on the responsibility to preserve this precious and limited treasure.

Instead of passing unenforceable laws, it is important that divers become educated about the cause and effect relationship we have with the ocean. You will find yourself a lot more caring and interested, once you learn about the contents of this "underwater art gallery" and its endless array of marine life.

Familiarize yourself with the names of the critters which inhabit this world. Which ones are common, which ones are rare, what kind of fish inhabit deeper water, discover their feeding habits and their preferred environment. Learn how to avoid stressing the marine life. For example: chasing turtles, lobsters, pufferfish or any other animal, can lower their defense capacity, thus making them more vulnerable to attack from their predators.

There are several books on marine life identification that will guide you in the identification process. Most boats have a library and will often present on-board marine life slide shows. If available, we highly recommend taking a Marine Awareness or Underwater Naturalist course which will not only show you how to find the name of the animals, but where to look for the fish or critters underwater. You will also learn which species are endemic to the area and which ones can be found at other destinations. The more you know about the marine environment, the more you can pass on to other divers, thus becoming an ambassador for Planet Ocean.

There are other factors, which will contribute to the conservation of the reef environment. These are often controlled by dive operators, but are important for you to be aware of.

Anchoring/Mooring

More and more dive boats are using permanent moorings. Unfortunately placing adequate moorings in remote locations can create difficult logistics and a considerable expense. If a vessel needs to anchor, it should be in a location with a rubble bottom or sand to avoid damage to the coral. As the dive industry progresses, these practices are becoming common place.

Fish Feeding

In many locations you'll see divemasters feed fish, eels or even sharks. It sure makes for a good underwater show, and underwater photographers and reef sightseers get a special thrill when non domesticated animals come close enough to take food. Granted these practices make for an exciting dive adventure, but the down side is, it usually changes the local reef ecosystem. When fish are fed on a regular basis, their natural behavior changes. Aggressive fish often chase away the more timid ones, resulting in a reef dominated by a few "bully" species.

In addition, feeding fish often creates a feeding frenzy, in which fish, particularly eels and sharks may direct their aggression toward the diver, accidentally mistaking fingers for food. Fish feeders must take responsibility for themselves. Don't blame the fish. Be aware that even though you may not be directly involved with the feeding process, a normally shy animal in its quest to join the frenzy, may see one of your fingers and mistake it for a free snack. It's a good idea to keep your hands and fingers protected and close to your body during these underwater shows.

Then, there is the additional concern about the effects on water quality. Often the containers, the fish food was kept in, such as plastic bags, get left behind, polluting the water and creating a new hazard for marine life.

In some areas, where fish have learned to feed from friendly divers, spear fishermen have taken advantage of the easily approachable fish and have killed whole populations of marine life.

By learning to understand the **natural** ecosystem of the reef, and appreciate the fish behavior in its **natural** state, you'll enhance your diving enjoyment on pristine virgin dive sites considerably. One relatively simple skill to learn, is how to spot cleaning stations. Here marine life can often be observed from very close up performing a natural, very interesting behavior.

Cleaning behavior is probably one of the most common symbiotic relationships in the tropical oceans. Cleaning stations are often detected by the behavior of the "customers." Look for fish hovering in one spot, fish in unusual positions, or even lined up in queues. On some occasions you may see pelagic fish, such as manta rays, sharks, or even turtles being cleaned by wrasses, angelfish or tangs.

Almost all fish visit cleaning stations regularly, including small tangs, large groupers, sharks, mantas and even turtles. While in "cleaning mode," these critters will often allow divers to approach closely, allowing for unique photographs and observation opportunities. Watch very closely and you may even see the cleaner enter the mouth or gills of its host.

With knowledge and patience, we as divers have the unique opportunity to not only visit the underworld, but to gently interact with its numerous inhabitants in a positive and constructive way. *Remember, YOU do make a difference.*

Underwater Photography

Live-Aboards offer the ultimate in photo logistics, education and opportunities. In fact, many of them have been designed by underwater photographers. Most vessels are laid out to make handling of photo equipment hassle free. Charging stations for batteries and other accessories are readily available. Camera tables make changing film and set up simple. With the assistance of a photo pro, which many modern vessels have available, competent divers can quickly learn to capture stunning underwater photographs.

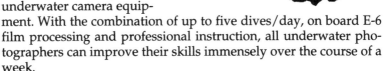

Beginners are always amazed at the results that can be achieved with todays modern underwater camera equipment. With the combination of up to five dives/day, on board E-6 film processing and professional instruction, all underwater photographers can improve their skills immensely over the course of a week.

Being able to view your processed film on-board, within 3-24 hours, is an invaluable necessity. Quality photographs don't happen by accident. It takes education and repetition to master underwater photography.

It is common for a Live-Aboard photographer to shoot up to 15-20 rolls in a week of diving. This "crash" course allows for the new photographer to build a strong foundation in the mechanical use of the camera, proper exposure settings and photo composition.

There is no better platform available to divers to get launched into the exciting world of underwater photography. The convenience of having your photo lab above you on the surface can make the difference when it comes to getting that rare shot. Many times we have run out of film at the same time we spotted a rare animal close to the boat. Fortunately we were able to get up on the boat, change tanks, load a new roll of film and go back down to get the shots.

A popular option to learn underwater photography, is to sign up for a trip with a "named" expert in U/W photography. Instructors such as: Jim Church, Scott Frier, Stephen Frink, Chris Newbert and ourselves, at Blue Kirio, all teach photo seminars to various levels of photographers. We have found that each photo instructor has a different style of shooting, and a different style on teaching a class. Some are very hands on and will dive with you assisting you with positioning and feedback from their observations, while others will take more of a classroom approach and place corrections in while reviewing your processed film. In order to get a well rounded picture of the many techniques and styles, you may want to attend a variety of courses and seminars.

• How do you know, when you're ready for this totally new approach to scuba diving?

Ask yourself, how comfortable you are in the water. Learning underwater photography requires concentration, so SCUBA diving should be almost second nature. If you still have to constantly fiddle with your dive gear, taking an additional piece of equipment, such as a camera, is definitely going to make things worse. One of the most important skills you should master before you get into underwater photography, is your buoyancy control.

It is essential, that you're able to consistently maintain neutral buoyancy. To capture good photographs, you can't be constantly bobbing up and down

51

and fussing with your dive gear. At the same time, since underwater photographers often need to get close to the bottom, poor buoyancy skills often result in damage to the reef. One way to reduce the likelihood of "kicking the reef" is to bend your knees and keep your fins off the reef, when you're doing close up photography.

Avoid touching the coral. If absolutely necessary, look for a rock or a piece of dead coral, to hold on to. Often, all you need is one finger, to stabilize yourself, for an extreme close up shot. But better yet, control your buoyancy so that you hover just **above** the reef.

If you're at all in doubt, whether you're ready for underwater photography, try carrying a large flashlight, or an empty crate, which would be very comparable in size to a housed camera, with you on your next dive. Treat this object as if it is a fragile camera. If you don't bang it around and are able to move efficiently while staying off the reef, then you are probably skilled enough to dive with a camera. Till then, stick to observing and honing your skills.

There are two basic types of systems that are commonly used by underwater photographers. The first one is simply a camera designed specifically for U/W use such as a Sea & Sea Motormarine or a Nikonos. The other choice is to place a quality land camera, such as a Nikon 8008s or a Cannon EOS model, in a specially designed underwater housing.

• Which system is the best? Good question.

Unfortunately there is no simple answer. Each system has its strengths and weaknesses. It becomes a matter of trade offs and compromises. If you can afford to, you may want to own both systems.

• If you're just beginning, you should rent a system.

Housed cameras are very seldom available for rent, so your best choice will be the Nikonos or Sea & Sea system. These systems are relatively easy to handle and give high quality results. The Nikonos is considered to be optically superior to the Sea & Sea, but carries a price tag which is substantially more. Generally, you get what you pay for with photo equipment.

Whichever system you start with, expect it to take at least a few dives to get used to handling the camera underwater, while maintaining buoyancy, buddy contact and equalized ears. With experience, you should become familiar with the system's strengths and weaknesses and how to competently dive with it.

Although designed with high quality optics, the Nikonos system holds a disadvantage to the housed camera system, when it comes to close-up and macro formats. With the Nikonos, you need to use either an extension tube and a fixed framer or a close up lens and a fixed framer to take pictures of small marine life. The subject you want to photograph needs to be placed within the framer. This works great for shells, starfish and other slow moving creatures, but creates an impossible task with most species of fish.

One of the major strengths of the Nikonos system is in its ease of use and high quality results when it comes to wide angle photography. Designed with the finest optics and large view finder, the Nikonos 15mm and 20mm lenses can provide outstanding images. Since this camera is a small and easy to maneuver system, we often choose the Nikonos for wide angle fish and reef photography, as well as for *Bluewater photography*.

Housed cameras require more "tinkering" with set-ups and are often larger and more cumbersome!!!

So what's the advantage???

By housing one of the advanced SLR (Single Lens Reflex) land cameras, you bring highly advanced electronic functions, autofocus, sophisticated metering and a wide selection of lens choices underwater. Also, in contrast to the Nikonos, you'll have the ability to see, focus and compose through the lens. What you see is pretty much what you get.

With a housing, you will find it also much easier to approach and photograph skittish marine life. This is a major factor if you, like most divers, want to take good fish portraits. Lenses such as the 60 or 105mm are the most popular for close-up photos. For wide angle you can place anything from a 20mm - 14mm lens in your port. We prefer housed cameras for fish portraits, most macro photography, *Bluewater photography* with shy subjects and *Above & Below photography*.

• Slide film or print film?

Many divers who have told us they are waiting to get good at underwater photography before they shoot slides. Well, for them, it will never happen. With print film you get variable exposures, and seldom an accurate representation of your photography. The quality of slides is by far superior to print film, and that's why all professionals use slide film.

Another important advantage of slide film (except Kodachrome) is you can process the film on-board most Live-Aboards. As we mentioned before, the instant feedback you receive, combined with unlimited diving and photo opportunities, is the key to learning underwater photography. This is why so many top photo professionals run their seminars aboard Live-Aboards.

If you're a beginner photographer, you should develop all your film on board to increase your learning potential. If you're a more experienced photographer, you should at least process a few rolls to check your equipment and general exposure settings. We recommend you process a roll, or two, at the start of the trip and at least one in the middle of your trip. By doing this you will be able to discover any equipment problems that may arise as the trip progresses. It's possible for a strobe to malfunction and be undetectable until you process the film.

There is nothing worse than shooting twenty rolls of film, only to find out, when you process it back home, that your strobe was not synchronized to your shutter. Even though it may cost more to process film on the boat, it's a lot cheaper than having to come back to the destination to shoot all the photos again.

Since a dive boat in the tropics has a difficult time maintaining the same high level standards that a professional lab back in America can, some professionals choose to process when at home. For the most part the quality of the processing procedures is good aboard and only the very discriminating eye can tell any difference in the processed film. As long as the photo pro is knowledgeable about storing, mixing, controlling temperature and changing of the chemicals, the processing quality should be fine.

• Types of film

There's a popular rule of thumb when it comes to selecting film: choose the slowest film possible for the lighting conditions. That way you will be guaranteed the finest grain, highest sharpness, and most vivid colors. Most U/W photographers select both 50ASA and 100ASA. Generally, most underwater photographers will shoot 100ASA for wide angle and 50ASA or less for macro. Since underwater photographers try to get close to their subject and utilize strobes as their major light source, they are able to get great results using these slower, less grainy films.

If you do plan to utilize on-board E-6 processing you should purchase either *Fujichrome* or *Ektachrome*. Fuji's most popular film is *Velvia*. This is an excellent 50ASA speed film for close-up photography. Fuji's *Sensia* and Provia are rated 100ASA and are favored for wide angle. Kodak's *Elite 100* and *Lumina* are also excellent film choices.

For films which are not processed on the boats, Kodak *Kodachrome 64* has long been the choice of many professionals for both wide angle and close up photography. For brilliant macro photos, *Kodachrome 25ASA* can produce superior results, but is a very slow film and requires an experienced user for consistent quality results.

• Buying your equipment

Minimum set up includes:

- camera body (plus housing if necessary)

- lenses (plus a port if for a housed camera)

- U/W lighting system (strobe)

- strobe cord

- arms and tray to mount strobes and camera

Once you decide what to buy you must shop around for it. The best prices are usually out of the mail order houses. You can find them listed in most photography magazines.

** **Beware:** Most mail order companies can be difficult to deal with if you are unsure of what you want. Few of the sales people really know anything about U/W photography and we have heard of many nightmare experiences of divers getting the wrong items. If you choose this route, you must have the part numbers for all the items or at least know exactly what you want.

If you are unsure of the particulars of a system, you should check with whoever has given you U/W photo instruction in the past. If you plan to travel with a photo specialist, seek their advise on particulars.

• Blue Water Photography

Blue water is usually referred to as water too deep to see the bottom, often thousands of feet deep. The attraction is to see forms of marine life you don't normally observe on the reef, such as oceanic sharks, whales, dolphins, pelagic gamefishes and pelagic jellyfish - just to name a few. Many times Blue Water photography is done while snorkeling, due to the disturbance in the water that SCUBA bubbles make. Marine life such as dolphins and whales

tend to shy away from the bubbles of a SCUBA diver. Since you are relatively close to the surface and more than six feet from these large subjects, strobes are seldom used. Blue Water SCUBA diving can be very tricky since there are no visual references for depth orientation. This is considered highly advanced diving. The use of a shark cage is common when diving in an area with large predators.

• Above & Below

Above & Below photography involves a housed camera system with a dome port. Attempting to capture both the underwater world and the top side

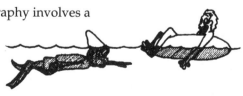

into one frame can be very tricky and difficult, but the images can be extremely rewarding and unusual. When shooting this type of photography it is very important to have a calm surface. The use of mask defogger or RainX will keep the water drops from forming on the upper half of the port. The shallower the water and closer the background subject, the better the photo. This type of photography generally requires the use of a split diopter in order to achieve focus throughout the depth of field.

• Macro and Fish Photography

In order to achieve a 1-1 ratio in macro photography, you will need to use a fixed lens as opposed to a zoom. Lenses such as the 50mm, 60mm 100mm, 105mm and 200mm produce the best results when using a housed camera. Small subjects provide challenges. Many are either highly camouflaged and/or shy and fast swimmers. Some bottom dwelling fish are easily photographed, once you find them. Others are colorful and easily spotted, but require a lot of patience to get close to. If you hover motionless and try to blend into the reef, you'll find that many fish get used to the diver's presence and continue their normal behavior. Note how they react to your exhalation and try to time your breathing so that you approach them while inhaling. Marine life is very sensitive to movement in the water and when you exhale, the bubbles usually scare the fish away. With a gentle breathing pattern and a great deal of patience, you may find that some fish become curious about divers, and move in closer, to "check you out." Keep in mind that your lens resembles the eye of a giant fish, and often scares fish more than the diver himself.

• Wide Angle Photography/Models

We recommend the Nikonos V with a 20mm or 15mm lens, or a housed camera with a 20mm lens or wider. Wide Angle photos allow you to capture a reef scene while still being close enough to light up the colorful marine life. Since even the most powerful strobes have little effect past 3 - 4 feet, it is important to approach close to the subject in order to bring out the true colors.

Although you can get excellent results by photographing reef scenes or schools of fish in their natural state, you may sooner or later try to add a model. The hardest part can be to find a dive buddy who's willing to model. Other underwater photographers make excellent models (as long as they leave their own camera behind), because they understand the elements of photography and are more likely to know what you're trying to accomplish. On a Live-Aboard, you can often talk one of the crew into modeling on some of the dives for you.

If your model is unfamiliar with underwater photography, you probably will need to coach him/her in the basic body positions and underwater signals. It is most important, that you discuss underwater communication before your dive. Develop signals to tell your model when to breath, what body, head and eye position you need, etc. You must realize underwater modeling is actually

"work" requiring a lot of patience on your part and the model's. If you ask your "better half" to be your model, you better be sure he or she is really interested in modeling for you. Unhappiness underwater can often carry over to well after your dive, potentially spoiling your dive vacation Remember, unless you're a professional photographer, you're on vacation!!!

• What to do with your photographs ?

Once you get "hooked" on underwater photography, you will most likely find yourself spending a lot of time, money and patience in order to improve your photographic skills. So what are you going to do with all these images? First of all, you should organize your slides into three categories:

1) Your best shots
2) Your " seconds ." Keep them for slide shows, or consider cropping them. If the slide is well focused, you can often turn an "o.k." shot into a great shot. (You can duplicate the slide and have the duplicate cropped, or have a print produced and crop the print).
3) Those which are trash. But don't throw them out, these are the ones you often learn the most from. Be sure to review them and determine what went wrong.

Once you've made your selection and categorized your shots, store your slides in quality slide pages (available at most photo stores). Be sure to keep them either in hanging files or three ring binders. Also place them away from heat, dampness and humidity.

• Making Prints

Many new photographers tend to want to get prints done of at least all their "best shots." You'll end up spending lots of money on prints which most likely end up in a dark closet. Be selective. Keep in mind, every tiny flaw on your slide, will appear exaggerated on your print. Consider picking just a few slides, possibly have them cropped, if at all required, and have a quality enlargement made.

We have found that the **Type R** prints provide very nice results for a reasonable price. If you choose to spend a little more money, the **Cibachrome** prints are custom made prints providing excellent quality and hold up well over time.

• Slide Shows

If you decide to select your "best shots" to share with friends and family on the screen, you should get duplicates done for projection. You can easily damage a slide (due to the heat of the projector bulb) during repeated use in slide shows. If you continue to use them in a slide projector, they also lose some of their color saturation.

• Publication

If you feel your images are just as good as those you see in the magazines, you may want to attempt to get them published. Select slides with excellent sharpness and exposure. Study the magazines you're planning on submitting to and try to meet their needs. Some magazines have a special feature, such as "Your favorite photo," or "My best shots." If accompanied by the appropriate text or story, the chances that your photos will be accepted, are more likely. Submit your slides in the same type of slide pages we suggested for storing. You can put each slide into a slide sleeve for added protection if you like. Don't forget your name, address and phone number, as well as a brief description of the subject and the location.

• Photo Contests

Study dive magazine for advertised photo contests. Some of the Live-Aboard operators, such as the Aggressor Fleet frequently arrange photo contests for their customers. If your image becomes placed, it usually gets

published in a popular dive magazine and you may win a prize. Requirements for submission differ. Read the directions well. Should you submit a slide or print? Are duplicates accepted? Will the image be returned to you? Generally speaking, you will need to send a self addressed stamped envelope to have your submission returned to you.

One word of caution to all beginning underwater photographers!!!

This activity can be very addicting and force you to want to travel the worlds oceans in search of that rare and unique prize winning photo!!!

..............Remember, we warned you.............

Additional Live-Aboard Tips and Etiquette

• Dehydration

Dehydration begins the night before your Live-Aboard dive trip. Maybe you're staying up late the night before your departure to celebrate with a few cold ones, followed by a caffeine beverages in the morning to help get through last minute packing. You're likely to load up on coffee for your run to the airport and the "big drain" just continues from there.

Since both alcohol and caffeine dehydrate the body, you'll be losing more fluid than you're taking in. The air conditioning in the airport and plane is moisture free and cold, a condition which, unfortunately, is hard for your body to process. Of course the dehydration process goes on, while diving. All divers know the feeling of "cotton mouth." The hot tropical climate doesn't help either.

To worsen the situation, some divers take medication, such as decongestants which also are dehydrating. Dehydration is known to contribute to decompression sickness, while severe dehydration is considered a medical emergency. Less obvious cases can cause accelerated exhaustion, leg cramps, a decline in your ability to respond, as well as a tendency to quickly become irritable.

There's only one solution: Plenty of water. The International Sports Medicine Institute recommends that you drink at least a half-ounce of water per pound of body weigh per day, under normal circumstances. When you add the exertion of diving and the

63

fact that you're breathing ultra dry air, you'll need a lot more fluid than that. Experts recommend that you drink at least a half-liter of fluid (water or juice, no caffeine beverages) before every dive.

• Sun Protection or "slip, slop and slap"

Yes, you've probably heard it before, but the sun does damage your skin, cause premature aging and can cause skin cancer. Traveling to trop- ical destinations, staying continuously "on the water" aboard Live-Aboards, multiplies the impact of the sun's ultraviolet (UV) rays.

So, when choosing your next Live-Aboard, keep in mind, the often still promoted "sun deck," may end up a dead space for most of the day, unless you do wish to become a "Kentucky-fried chicken." At the same time you probably don't want to spend all your surface intervals inside the air conditioned interior of the boat. So, when requesting a brochure of the Live-Aboards you're considering to travel on, look for covered exterior areas.

Meanwhile stick to the Australian rule: "Slip, slop, slap." Slip on a shirt, slop on some sunscreen and slap on a hat.

• Camera Table Etiquette.

Many of Live-Aboard cruisers have a specially designed table or at least a space set aside for underwater photographers to work on their photo gear. Since the camera table is often located in a con- venient location on the dive deck, it can easily become, a "catch all." Often tens of thousands dollars worth of camera equipment are stored on this table. We have found that the following guide- lines can often alleviate frustration and potential disasters:

1) Don't leave open drinks on the table.

2) Don't leave food on the table or eat food from the table.

3) Don't leave towels and T-shirts on the camera table. Cameras can get pulled off the table, if someone picks up the towel/T-shirt carelessly.

4) Don't smoke near the camera table.

• Dip Tanks

A freshwater dip tank or bucket is usually made available for cameras and computers only. It is important that the water doesn't become contaminated. Please don't dip masks with defog etc., in this body of freshwater. It could harm the camera's lenses. If you need to rinse something off try the deck shower or ask for a mask bucket.

• Briefings

Listen carefully, when the crew does the trip briefing. You may have heard the emergency procedures before, but keep in mind Live-Aboards are not as standardized as planes, and most procedures vary greatly from the boat you were on last. Each ocean, each dive site is different. Briefings are designed to make your trip and each dive safe, smooth and enjoyable.

• Freshwater Conservation

The instructor who taught your open water course and "the book" probably told you, if you don't rinse your gear religiously after every dive you'll ...die!!

Well.... as all seasoned Live-Aboard divers can tell you, if your gear is under constant use, (3-5) dives a day, then it's not a problem to rinse it only at the end of the trip. Most of your equipment remains damp during the entire trip, so salt crystals are less likely to form. You might want to rinse off your camera gear, dive computer and second stages after each dive, but although most Live-Aboards have desalinization, (procedure that filters sea water into pure drinking water), freshwater is somewhat limited and won't last through the trip, if each diver constantly rinses off their gear.

Communications

The vast majority of Live-Aboards are equipped with modern communication devices such as a Single Sideband (SSB) or Very High Frequency (VHF) radio. Most vessels have some form of shore based support that can assist in the case of any emergency. Some boats even have cellular communications so you can make phone calls and send faxes from the boat. With more and more "cells" going in around the world, travelers are finding cellular phones can be used from some very remote destinations. If you have a phone and think you may use it, take it, and you may get lucky. If cellular service is available and you have the right adapter, you can even send faxes from your computer. Of course, the expense of this is variable.

If no cellular system exists, radio telephone calls are also available, but can be costly. If you know you need to make a call while on the boat, let the captain know in advance and he can advise you of all the logistics and cost. Some vessels travel through areas where the communication is spotty or blocked out entirely. The sooner the captain knows of your request the better he can arrange the boat to be in a place where there will be a guaranteed communication link.

For vessels located in more remote regions of the world, you could possibly send/receive faxes via the vessel's local shore based office. It does require a considerable effort and expense by several people to pass the information along by radio or skiff messenger so please request this service only when it's very important.

If you have to be in constant communication with someone back home, then you're better off at a landbased resort or on a Live-Aboard closer to home. Before giving family members the numbers to contact you in case of a family emergency, consider the logistics of how you could attend to the emergency when you're thousands of miles away. Most of the time you will be far offshore without a quick and easy connection to the nearest airport. Often the

flights in and out of remote destinations occur only once a week. Under these circumstances you may want to just put all the "good or bad news" on hold, until you get back to civilization.

On the day the boat returns to port you can usually access a phone or fax machine via a local hotel. Expect to pay up to $6 per page.

Seasickness

Modern Live-Aboards are generally large stable ships, and not subject to as much motion as smaller day charter boats, making seasickness somewhat of a rare occurrence. Still, some people are more prone to seasickness than others and may have to deal with temporary discomfort. However, divers who commonly get sick on small boats often find themselves unaffected on the larger Live-Aboards. If you consider yourself prone to sea-sickness choose a destination with no island crossings and/or travel at the time of the year when the water is likely to be calmest.

The simple physiological rea-son a person suffers from motion sickness is that there is a discrepancy between what the eyes see, and what the ears feel. This confusing information causes the brain to send a message of imbalance, thus giving the person a feeling of nausea. There are also other factors that tend to add to seasickness. However, most of these elements can easily be eliminated:

- lack of food

- too much sun

- lack of rest

- overindulgence in alcohol / dehydration

- "pre-dive" nerves

- any conditions that deplete the body's normal strength level

Usually, as divers become accustomed to the motion, the symptoms will subside. Most divers are fine after the first night's rest.

Preventive Measures

There are many over the counter drugs that help relieve motion sickness, such as *Dramamine, Bonine, Maalox, Triptone* and others. They seem to work best if you start treatment 12-24 hours before the ship's departure.

Be aware that many of these drugs have side affects, such as drowsiness.

Your doctor can also prescribe *Scopolamine*. A patch that you attach to your skin, with the medicine absorbed through the skin. This one can have some strong side affects and should be used with caution. For more information on prescription drugs available, check with your doctor.

There are also some natural medicinal methods to fend off seasickness that have proven quite effective.

Ginger root seems to work real well for many people. Ginger root pills are available, or, grind fresh ginger and drink it as a tea with hot water, (add honey if you like).

One of the most effective non medicinal methods we are aware of, are "Sea Bands." These are elastic bands that apply accupressure to a point that seems to relieve nausea, due to seasickness. Developed by the British Navy, these little wonders have been out on the market for a number of years.

If you find yourself getting seasick in spite of preventative measures, or because none are available, you should lie down and sleep, if possible. If you can't sleep, stay out in the fresh air and try to concentrate either on the horizon or a land mass close by. Position yourself toward the center of the vessel on the lowest deck possible. Place a cold towel behind your neck. Eat and drink as much as you stomach will allow (avoid greasy food), to keep your strength up. If the boat is at anchor, you may just go for a swim or snorkel. This eliminates the motion for a while and may help you overcome seasickness.

Meals Aboard

Generally the food is varied and plentiful. Fresh vegetables and fruits are the norm along with poultry, beef, pork and fresh seafood. The cook on a Live-Aboard is usually the busiest person on the boat, resulting in three main meals and plenty of snacks, such as brownies, cookies, nachos and lots of other good stuff. Divers like to eat and most vessels make food quality and quantity a top  priority. Usually guests find the menu to their liking.

Special Menu Request

If you do require a special menu or food type, you can usually be accommodated. Some Live-Aboard operators will send you a dietary request form. If they don't, you can send a note stating your dietary needs. It is not uncommon for divers to have special requests. Some are health related, while others represent a "wish list." If you seriously need special food, or are allergic to something, then you need to point that out clearly ahead of time. Double check with the boat's chef upon your arrival and **before the boat's departure**. The messages don't **normally** get passed on from the office to the boat. It is also possible that the cook overlooked your request.

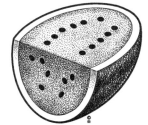

Keep in mind, that in some remote locations, many of the food items we take for granted here in the modern world, are just not available. It is not uncommon to travel to a beautiful tropical island destination and find that fresh fruit and vegetables are not available. Diet soda can also be a luxury. Whatever you want, it's ok to ask, but don't expect everything to be available. Flexibility is the key.

If you want to start your diet, wait until you return home. We often see special requests for low fat, low salt meals from a guest, who is the first to eat a cheese burger and ignore the special meal the cook prepared just for them. We are never surprised to see the low fat eaters go for the chocolate cake after a night dive.

If you truly want or need a special meal, then show the cook your appreciation by eating it. As we stated before, dive boat cooks have the busiest job on any quality boat. They often double as housekeepers, divemasters and deckhands. Don't make their job harder by having them prepare an extra meal if it's not going to be eaten.

Once the boat has left port, there is (normally) no more shopping available. Make sure you pack a supply of your favorite candy, a special tea you can't live without, your powdered cappuccino, or anything else you feel you cannot miss for the duration of the trip.

Packing

When embarking on a dive adventure there are a lot of packing details to sort out. Since SCUBA diving is such an equipment intensive sport, and space on a boat is limited, it is important to take just what you will really need and will use.

Remember that airlines **do** have baggage size and weight restrictions, and can and will charge hefty excess baggage fees. With small airlines, you can almost always count on tight restrictions and enforcement of the policies. Large  international carriers generally allow two checked bags limited to 70 pounds each. Carry-on is usually one bag at no more than 10 pounds (seldom will anyone weigh your carry-on bag, provided it is not obviously overweight and/or bulky).

Smaller regional carriers often have checked weight restrictions of less than 60 pounds *total*. For instance, it is very possible to fly into Fiji with 130 plus pounds of luggage only to find you will need to pay an additional several hundred dollars to get all your gear to the Solomons. We suggest you get the latest up-to-date information from *each* airline you will be traveling with.

• Packing Tips

Since dress is usually quite casual on-board, don't take too many clothes. Consider a set of nice casual clothes for travel and one for the departure night party and a sweatshirt for chilly nights. But, most of the time you will find yourself in swimsuits and shorts. You can always rinse a T-shirt or shorts out and dry them in the sun. Generally, novice Live-Aboard divers overpack.

When packing, figure that one set of dive gear will take up the better part of one bag. Add a few swimsuits, shorts and T-shirts, and your second check-in bag will start to fill. Most divers have no problem staying under the airline restrictions, but for U/W photographers it can be a nightmare.

When we pack for a dive trip we always have a bathroom scale close by to check the weight of our bags.

Most divers use soft sided bags to carry their gear. These bags can easily be folded up and stored on any boat. When looking for a quality bag, we recommend bags such as the *Oceanic Divepak*. Since all compartments are accessed through a single large opening, this extremely durable full size bag (backpack style), can be easily locked.

Ocean Edge also has a nice backpack as well as a no gimmick duffel bag, which may not be quite as durable, but is convenient to pack and carry.

If your looking for a top of the line bag and money is no object, *Seaware* makes perhaps the most durable bags, utilizing *Ballistics wearcoat*, an extremely long lasting material. As with most things, you get what you pay for.

There are many other dive gear bags on the market, and you might find one more suitable for your needs and budget, but keep in mind, that the more gadgets, zippers, pockets on the bag, the more prone to breakage they are.

For divers looking for a large (but not too large) case that is legal under most airline policies and durable for fragile dive and photo equipment, we recommend the use of a 24 gallon "Action Packer" (# 1172), which you can purchase from stores, such as K-Mart for under $25.00. **Note:** *Not always practical when traveling on a small boat with little storage space.*

These inexpensive cases are well suited to carry all your sensitive dive and photo gear, along with other things. Although we pack camera bodies and sensitive lenses and ports into our carry-on, we find the Action Packer to be an excellent case for strobes, housings, trays, arms, etc. Action Packers are capable of carrying the weight needed and are tough enough to protect sensitive equipment if packed properly.

When packing, place a few inches of foam, wetsuit or a few layers of clothes on the bottom and any sensitive gear toward the middle of the case. Line the outer edge with foam or pad with clothes. Place soft items such as T-shirts, shorts, towels etc., between packed items to further protect them. Stuff film, clothes, and other small items in the "dead spaces," such as the inside of a housing.

Under normal traveling conditions, this method of packing works well. To lock the Action Packer, use plastic ties for the handles and, in addition, duct tape the whole case. Ice chests are an alternative, but are more expensive, bulkier and have more weight to start with. However, it's easy to install hinges on one side, making it very convenient for locking purposes.

Though some dive bags do come equipped with attached wheels, often they seldom last for more than a few trips. Much more reliable and practical are the sturdy *Concord luggage carts.* We recommend at least seize # 2, to hold up the weight of dive and camera equipment. Personally we prefer seize # 3. Larger than that, they become a little inconvenient to carry on. Approximate cost: $75-$90.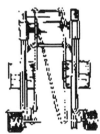

• Carry-on

We prioritize our carry-on as items that are small and compact, expensive, difficult to immediately replace or substitute for, and vital to the success of our trip. There are many legal sized bags which will allow you to carry on items such as: your regulator, computer (personal and dive), camera body, lenses, change of clothes, toiletries and your sole supply of any medication you absolutely must have. Checked in luggage can get delayed and even lost. It is important that you plan in advance to insure only a "minor inconvenience" instead of a "major disaster" if it happens to you. The inconvenience of hauling a carry on through the airport is a small price to pay for the peace of mind that comes with knowing the most important items will arrive safe and on-time. Renting a BCD or pair of fins is often less troublesome than dealing with someone's poorly tuned rental regulator.

• If you forget ...

...your passport: you will find out when you attempt to check in for your flight. Airlines will not issue a boarding pass to anyone without a valid passport for overseas flights. If you are in your home city, you might have time to get home to collect it or, if a friend or relative has access to your house, they may be able to deliver it to you at the airport, or send it by a courier service. If you are many hours away from your home, the only alternative, besides canceling the trip, is to stay in a hotel for a day and have your passport delivered express mail/Fed Ex to you. Again, this requires someone having access into your home and having exact directions of where to find your passport. Then, you can catch a flight the following day to your destination. Of course this only works if there is a flight the following day and the boat is able to pick you up a day late, *(see Booking your trip)*.

...your airline ticket. As long as you have the ticket number available (photocopy ticket), most airlines can re-issue your ticket for a small fee, (approximately $60.).

...your certification card. Fax or call the agency in the country which certified you with your full name and date of birth. As long as you contact them during office hours they will fax back to confirm your certification. This can usually be done from the Live-Aboard (see communication), or the vessel's skipper can radio the land based support office and they will forward the request to your certification agency.

The following checklist was designed so you won't leave **anything important** behind. You may find some items don't apply to you and may want to customize the list to meet your own personal needs. The purpose is to give you a check list to start with.

DIVERS TRAVEL CHECK LIST

• Necessary Gear
(be sure all gear is clearly marked with your name)

[] Mask, snorkel, fins
[] Booties
[] Regulator
[] BCD
[] Alternate Air source
[] Dive Computer
[] Exposure suit
[] Dive light (required for night diving)
[] Gear bag

• Recommended Additional Gear

[] Backup dive computer
[] Compass
[] Dive knife
[] Gloves
[] Weight belt (no weight)
[] Dive Slate
[] Log book
[] Any photo equipment
[] Spare batteries
[] Film or video tapes

• Documents
Photo copy all of the following documents and keep them separate

[] Valid Passport *(must be valid for a minimum of 6 months)*
[] Round trip airline tickets
[] Certification Card
[] Proof of medical insurance (DAN card)

[] Cash for miscellaneous travel expenses (One dollar bills for tips)
[] International calling card and a list of important phone numbers
[] Owners manual for new, complicated equipment

• Medical Kit Suggestions

[] Aspirin/Tylenol
[] Motion sickness medicine
[] Decongestants (Sudafed, Afrin)
[] Band-aids (various sizes)
[] Neosporine for coral cuts
[] Antibiotics (Ciprofloxacin works for
    many marine environment related infections,
    as well as for traveler's diarrhea)
[] Insect repellent
[] Sting relief medicine
[] Suntan lotion (non-oily)
[] Sunburn lotion (Aloe)
[] Swim Ear (Antibiotic)
[] Extra contact lenses

• Clothing and Personal Suggestions

[] T-shirts
[] Shorts
[] Swim suits
[] Sweatshirt or light weight jacket
[] Lightweight rain coat if the trip includes land excursions
[] Long pants
[] Toiletries including toothbrush
[] Sunglasses
[] Sun hat
[] Beach towel
[] Sandals or soft soled shoes. Hiking shoes if land excursions
    are offered
[] Presents for the crew and/or natives

• Entertainment

[] CDs
[] Tapes (music and/or video)
[] Walkman
[] Books
[] Fish ID books
[] Games (cards, chess, cribbage, electronic games)

Live-Aboard Selection

Deciding on which boat to travel on is like choosing your hotel, restaurant and dive shop all in one. In today's competitive dive market there are many choices when it comes to Live-Aboards.

But unlike hotels, which were designed for one purpose, most Live-Aboard dive boats have been converted from fishing or oil rig vessels to work as dive boats, hotels and a restaurant, all in one.

Recently some of the newer vessels have been custom built for this purpose from the ground up. These super luxury ships are very expensive to build and maintain. Though beautiful in design and function, their practicality over the years, based on their financial return, is questionable.

Live-Aboard designs vary from catamarans to trimerans to monohulls. Some are made of wood, with most of them built out of steel or aluminum. The vast majority are power vessels, while some are motor sailers. Size of the boats ranges from 30 feet to 170 feet, with passenger limits between four to over thirty passengers. Since few of the vessels where originally designed for SCUBA diving, you will find that there are trade offs and compromises to be made with each boat.

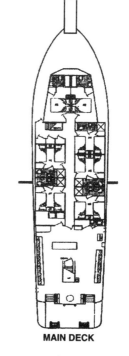

MAIN DECK

81

Small Live-Aboards (less than 65 feet) usually accommodate small intimate groups, but seldom sport the true luxury and stability that a large dive cruiser provides.

• So the question remains, which vessel is best for you?

When choosing a dive boat, our experience has taught us to carefully evaluate the trip logistics and the local diving and weather conditions. If we will be exposed to open ocean conditions, then the stability and sea worthiness of the boat becomes a high priority. The simple fact that small boats rock and roll much more than large vessels, thus making for an uncomfortable ride and possible seasickness and loss of sleep, leads us to consider larger vessels for areas where we will be making inter-island crossings. In destinations where our route takes us along a protected coastline, such as Kona, Hawaii, the size and sea worthiness of the ship is less of a concern.

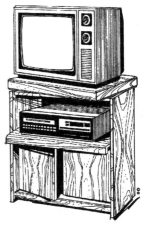

In regards to creature comfort, we look at larger boats that are more spacious, allowing for amenities such as vast quantities of fresh water, a wider selection of food, hot tub, private cabins, with shower and toilet facilities, entertainment centers (TV, VCR, stereo, etc...) and more quiet space to relax. These boats usually have well stocked photo departments and a spacious area to work on camera equipment. Of course all of this space and luxury comes with a higher price tag and generally more passengers.

Although there are exceptions, most small Live-Aboards provide "rustic" conditions by today's standards, due to the limitations on space, fresh water, privacy and food variety. Though not as fancy, these vessels have a strong appeal to many veteran divers who prioritize small groups and flexible itineraries. What they give up in privacy, they feel, is returned in the quality of the diving and price.

For divers who want the luxury larger vessels usually provide, combined with the flexibility of a small group of only 4-6 passengers, there are few small but luxurious Live-Aboards, which cater to this market. This type of vessel is new to the Live-Aboard industry and charters for about the same cost per diver as the larger ones. In areas where inter-island crossings are unnecessary, these vessels provide an excellent balance of luxury and small intimate groups.

Whatever your priorities, remember, you will need to choose a boat that you can live on for several days. It's important that you research the vessel so that you are not disappointed in the lack of comfort or find yourself with a large number of divers you didn't expect. You must decide on the degree of comfort you can live with.

For those of you who are new to Live-Aboards, you may want to pay a little extra and dive with a few more divers, from one of the larger vessels we have described.

• How many divers is comfortable on a Live-Aboard?

The number of passengers the vessel accommodates comfortably, really depends on the vessel's layout as well as size. On vessels where Mothership diving is practiced, you will find that any more than 16 divers can often lead to crowding on the dive site. Veteran divers avoid this problem by staggering their diving schedule to miss diving with the groups.

Vessels that run launches, allowing the divers to split up in small separate groups while diving, can comfortably accommodate a few more divers if organized properly. Here it is important not to drop all the divers at the same time on the same spot. Many vessels will stagger the time they drop off the divers or will even dive them in more than one dive site. Since it is safest to always have more than one tender on a current swept area, in case one boat's engine fails, or divers get carried away from the general dive sites and require "rescue," some operations insist on not splitting the tenders up.

We have found our **ideal** number on the vessels we have run and lead groups on to be between 14 and 18 people, depending on the vessel and local diving logistics. Having a fair number of divers on the boat helps create a positive social atmosphere top side. A big part of an adventure, is the people you encounter and meet along the way. It's fun to travel with a group who share a common interest. Often divers make friends with others during a trip and continue to travel together for years to come.

What are the differences between owner/operated vessels verses large corporate and/or franchised owned vessels ?

The large fleets, such as the Aggressor Fleet, are owned by either the corporation or private groups who have purchased a franchise, much like McDonalds or Burger King. These vessels are operated under a set of standards set up by the corporate office and attempt to maintain the same set of operating procedures throughout their organization and franchised boats. They are mostly supported by their own advertising and booking office and are fairly efficient in handling the day to day details of running a complex business. All of their bookings are processed through a main office and relayed to the appropriate ship's captain.

The captains, manage the vessel themselves and often handle all of the personal details except paychecks. The operating performance of each vessel is evaluated by the company based on customer feedback, as well as an annual inspection by the fleet manager. If there is a problem, they usually attend to it immediately and resolve it as quickly as possible.

If you have a complaint while aboard it should be addressed to the captain. If they fail to properly resolve the problem, you can then refer it to the fleet head office upon your return for additional assistance if needed. Over the years most of these companies have been very successful. Generally these fleet ships are financially stable and backed by the corporation. If they become financially strapped, damaged or sink, you are likely to get fully reimbursed.

Of course in the real world of Live-Aboard diving there can be some "leaks" in this system. The only potential weakness to this

operational structure is if the crew is new and unprepared or burned out and just putting in the time. As with any business, there are highly motivated employees and "slugs," (people who are either burned out or just don't understand the demanding energy that this job requires). As mentioned in the chapter "Gratuities," it's really the on-board crew who makes or breaks your trip.

Vessels managed by the owner usually have all of their finances tied up in the operation. Their business is based on their knowledge of the destination, personalized service provided and the operating condition of their vessel. Seldom do any of these owners operate a multi million dollar boat, but instead base their business on themselves providing divers with great diving, service and modestly comfortable boats.

If the vessel is captained by the owner(s), you usually find a more personalized touch in the organization of your charter. Captains who are the owners generally take a lot more pride in the vessel's reputation, and are usually there for the long haul. They are not subject to "others" rules and tend to be more flexible. If you have a complaint while aboard, you will be able to address the owner right on the spot. Often this system brings about a quicker solution to the problem. Many Live-Aboard owner/operators have an excellent reputation!

Though most of these small companies run a solid business, some of the less established operations often live charter to charter. If they run out of money, or cannot afford to make repairs, you may find yourself at the dock, in a far away country, with no boat in sight. We have heard of cases where divers lost their money because the boat had gone out of business for financial and/or other reasons before their arrival.

In these cases seldom does the diver see a refund. With any operation, especially overseas, it is imperative you check out their financial and political stability before you start any payments. Unless the Live-Aboard has established itself, you can't be sure if it will still be in operation by the time you get there.

Most owner-operated boats book through travel agents due to the time consuming process and the expense of corresponding overseas. Since the owner is on the boat and out to sea most of the time, they are unable to handle calls and mail efficiently.

• Tips on basic essential features to look for when choosing a Live-Aboard

- Spacious dive deck with individual space for dive accessories. Most will provide either baskets or built in lockers. Often you will find a camera table and fresh water showers on the dive deck.

- Easy diving access. Dive platforms for mothership diving which are large enough for two or more divers at a time and low enough to safely handle accessories such as cameras. If tender diving, it is important that the loading area is easy to handle tanks and other equipment and safe for passengers to load between boats.

- Private air conditioned cabins. Most boats have a central air conditioning system. The closer your room is to the cooling unit, the colder it will be. With these systems you seldom have any control regulating the temperature. Often you can restrict the flow of air, if your room is too cold, by adjusting the vents, or placing duct tape over them. The newer dive cruisers have individual AC units with controls that allow the guest to regulate the temperature in their individual stateroom.

- Fresh, hot and cold water showers. Some vessel are equipped with desalinators that can produce fresh water from salt. Others fill up at the beginning of the week and try to be conservative throughout the trip.

No matter what anyone advertises, there is no such thing as *unlimited* fresh water on a boat. Most desalinators only produce 45-60 gallons an hour. These desalinators are not designed to run all day. So the amount of water they actually produce is less than one would think. It doesn't take long for one to use up thousands of gallons of water if you take long showers and leave the water running while brushing your teeth.

*** *The rule on fresh water, on a boat is...BE CONSERVATIVE!!!*

- Charging stations for batteries and camera strobes (110 voltage).

- High crew to customer ratio. Generally speaking, the more crew members the more complete the service. This also makes operating the vessel safer if the weather was to turn rough.

- E-6 processing. If you are a photographer, on board E-6 processing is essential.

- Quality food. Divers like to eat. It is important to keep up the energy level while doing several dives a day over a period of days. Meals should be plentiful and variable.

- 24 hour a day electricity. This is important if you plan to charge accessories for diving. It also is a comfort if you need to get up at night and make your way about the boat.

The trend to comfort and luxury continues, and most of the modern Live-Aboards world wide, meet this standard, and in fact, surpass it. Staterooms with private toilets and showers, individual AC controls, hot tub, video monitor and entertainment centers are becoming the norm.

But with the increase of "bells and whistles" comes the increased odds of breakdown. Keep in mind that that these high maintenance vessels, with several mechanical systems, operate daily in the sun and salt water environment which can periodically lead to eventual system failures. Most operations carry back ups and generally can fix most problems. If this does occur to you on your trip, remember that your patience and understanding are greatly appreciated by the crew.

Choosing the Right Destination

When deciding on a destination you will enjoy, don't just take the recommendation of a friend, consider other factors such as:

Your experience level

Be sure you have the dive skills required to safely dive a particular destination. Novice divers should set themselves up for success by diving destinations that predominately produce mild diving conditions. There is no magic number of dives that indexes a divers skill level, but what we have found is that newer divers generally fair better on Live-Aboards located in destinations that are relatively close to the States. Not only is the diving in Hawaii, Bahamas, Cayman, and some of the other Caribbean destinations generally "easy" diving, but you will usually find the crew to speak English. Since most of them are either instructors or divemasters, they will be qualified to communicate to you the proper boat and dive procedures. It can be frustrating traveling to a destination where the language is hard to understand, especially if it's your first time on a Live-Aboard boat.

This is not to say that if you go to Australia you won't understand the boat's procedures. But why not set yourself up for long term diving success. Locations which involve long airline travel itineraries are generally associated with lack of sleep and jet lag. If you are unfamiliar with a Live-Aboard schedule, don't complicate it by making your first trip a long journey. If you are inexperienced, stick close to home and learn to walk before you run.

It's not fair to yourself and the boat crew to go to a place that has advanced diving when you have beginner experience. And please realize, that since you took an "Advanced course," and have now logged your 10th dive or so, you are on the right track - but you are still a beginner, when it comes to truly advanced diving destinations.

Your personal style of diving

Marine life encounters are influenced by one's own personal diving style. Divers who poke along the reef looking for small macro life, will have a very different diving experience than the diver who "cruises" the wall looking for "big stuff." If you were to interview a group of divers, who just ended a seven day dive trip on a Live-Aboard in, let's say, Papua New Guinea, you could hear opinions about the quality of diving as varied as:

"Great area for pelagica, I saw sharks, schools of eagle rays and a whale-shark."

Possibly pure luck. But most likely this diver cruises with the reef behind him, constantly looking into the blue water, including frequent glances toward the surface, as well as toward the bottom. Encounters with pelagics often involve swimming into currents and/or leaving the wall and actually swimming "into the blue," a dive style which demands a high level of experience.

"Nothing too special. Some large coral fans, couple of caves and your usual reef fish."

This is the typical comment of a diver who cruises along the wall, watching only what's in front of him. He'll miss the eagle ray above him, the school of barracudas hovering sixty feet off the reef, as well as the sharks below him. Unfortunately these divers usually move too fast to spot  "special" marine life such as tiny colorful nudibranches, camouflaged scorpionfish or pipefish and often lack the interest to learn fish identification, thus not knowing the difference between rare and common reef fish, reducing the excitement of "discovery."

"Tremendous variety of life. Leafy scorpionfish, rare dragonette fish, sharks...."

This diver most likely tends to slowly cruise the reef, carefully checking into every nook and cranny, without lacking to glance over the shoulder into the blue, to see what might be cruising by.

"Not much for pelagics, but great macro life!"

The comment of macro photographer, who's happy to spend his whole dive getting "the" shot of a clown fish, or shooting a roll of film on a nudibranch from all positions.

The bottom line is, when evaluating a dive destination, get more than one divers opinion and realize that *divers* tend to see the most of what *divers* are focused on seeing.

Personal priorities

What is your main interest? Remoteness, virgin reefs, large pelagics, array of offered dive classes? Small groups? Convenience in regards to airline connections? The luxury of the vessel? etc...

As you gain experience, your interests will probably change. At first you may want to take advantage of specialty classes offered by the vessel's on-board instructors. Especially if you haven't been able to gain a lot of experience yet, taking a class in, lets say drift diving in Palau or wreck diving in Truk Lagoon, can greatly enhance your safety and enjoyment in these more advanced destinations. The additional information and the individual instructor supervision might turn your dive trip from an o.k. experience into the vacation of a lifetime.

Later, you may want to take up underwater photography or videography. Then, you'll begin to judge each dive and each destination from a different prospective altogether.

Do you prefer close-up photography of unique, but tiny creatures? Or wide angle photography? A destination you explored as a beginner diver, and you thought you have "outgrown," could become attractive again, now that you are a photographer.

Is your non-diving spouse planning to accompany you?

Then, inspect the operation in regards to activities besides diving. Are land excursion offered? Are kayaks, windsurfers and other watersport equipment available? Are the reefs shallow enough to be attractive for snorkeling?

Are the buddy rule or the depth limitations an issue for you?

Boats in foreign countries, which are not U.S. owned, are generally more flexible with these rules, *(see "Buddy system")*.

Destinations: Definitions of Terms

In the following chapters we'll be describing many of the world's most popular Live-Aboard destinations. Since there are enough guides, brochure and articles, describing the beauty, endless visibility and never ending sunshine of each destinations, we have focused on pointing out specific facts that will make your trip preparation simple. By doing so, we want to prevent disappointments, and help you choose the destination which is right for you and your level of diving experience. We in no way want to discourage you from considering any of the destinations in your diving career. All of them are unique and worth visiting, as long as you are properly prepared.

Many of the vessels and destinations we've experienced personally, but others were recommended and/or described to us by tour leaders, world renown underwater photographers, world Live-Aboard travelers, and marine biologists, who have vast experience diving from some of the finest Live-Aboards throughout the world.

We suggest that you ask for the operator's brochure and check dive magazines and books, describing Live-Aboards in detail for color pictures and amenities and make a decision, utilizing the information in the guide. If you are prone to seasickness, choose a large stable ship, in areas with potentially rough water conditions, even if you think another boat looks prettier. If you decide to travel to a location during the rainy season, book onto a vessel with plenty of interior space. If you travel during the dry season, look for a big sundeck, or, if you are concerned about the effects of the tropical sun, make sure the boat of your choice has plenty of shaded deck area.

Topics to be included are:

Overview: The destinations lay out, highlights besides diving and other important aspects.

Location: Geographic location.

Airlines: Listing of the airlines which service this destination at the time of publication.

Airport: The nearest international airport you need to fly in to.

Climate: Temperatures are average only. In hot and humid climates, you'll find the temperatures to be much more pleasant on a Live-Aboard, due to constant ocean breezes.

Visibility: We provide you with the average visibility you can expect when experiencing normal weather conditions for the designated time of year. Plankton blooms are hard to predict and seasonal occurrences. They usually limit the visibility temporarily. In some areas whale sharks come to feed during plankton blooms. Otherwise the visibility depends, on tides (with the incoming tide usually providing for better visibility), on swells (surge stirs up sandy bottom), and rain (freshwater run off pollutes the water).

Water temperatures: Provides you with average water temperatures so you can choose the proper exposure protection. We recommend a 1/4" (7mm) wet suit with hood, when temperatures are in the 60's or even low 70's, a 3/16 " (5mm) wetsuit and a hood for night dives at temperatures from 72^0 F to 76^0 F, 1/8" (3mm) wetsuit and a thin hood for night dives at temperatures from 78^0 F to 82⁰ F and a lycra skin for temperatures above 82⁰ F for the average diver. If you get cold easily, adjust your choice of exposure suit accordingly.

Many divers assume all tropical locations feature water so warm, that a wet suit becomes unnecessary. But in spite of their tropical location, some areas, such as the Galapagos, which are located on the equator, are fed by cold currents (Humboldt current). Fiji and Papua New Guinea are generally perceived as very tropical, and although water temperatures rise as high as 86⁰ F in summer, they can drop to the low to mid 70's in winter. Now, that's still relatively warm, but if you're planning to do 4-5 dives a day, you'll soon wish you brought a full wet suit and maybe even a thin hood.

Crossings: If inter-island or open ocean crossings are involved, we recommend the use of a single hull, 100 foot plus aluminum or steel boat, if available. Since you are exposed to open ocean conditions, the seas can get very rough and uncomfortable. Multi-hulled vessels (catamarans and trimerans) tend to "slam" into the waves making for a very rough and sometimes dangerous crossings. Of course, if the water is calm, a bathtub is all one really needs.

Water condition: An important aspect, when choosing your Live-Aboard vessel. If the boat is seaworthy, traveling during the "off season" may be an option. Winter or monsoon storms can bring rain, large swells and wind. But there may be many weeks in between these natural occurrences where the water is flat as a lake and visibility outstanding. As long as you prepare for the worst, it's probably okay taking a bit of a chance. But remember, not to blame the captain, crew or fish for your bad luck with the weather.

Currents: If you are an inexperienced diver, save those destinations with strong currents until you had plenty of experience in destinations where mother ship diving is practiced and currents are uncommon. Generally the Caribbean and Hawaii offer great diving for beginners.

Diving topography: Information about the underwater terrain.

Note: Sheer walls with great visibility can be deceiving. It's easy to sink into the abyss. Generally, gradual sloping walls, with a shallower bottom are easier for beginners to judge depth and control buoyancy.

Reef structure: The type of corals and sponges.

Marine life highlights: The type of marine life you'll most likely remember. However in most locations, there's much more to see. Your marine life encounters will vary greatly with your style of diving, currents, time of the year, time of day, and tidal changes.

Of course there are some locations where you're more likely to see pelagics than others, and there are some destinations/dive sites which may have great macro life, but the currents are too strong for you to slow down enough to focus on a tiny shrimp. When talking about diving Cocos Island, most divers just refer to the sharks. Truth is, there are some excellent opportunities to view and photograph some rare and unusual macro life.

Night diving: Predominate marinelife and diving conditions.

Prime diving season: Though some boats do shut down for a couple of months a year due to seasonally poor weather conditions, many vessels are able to operate year round. Our definition of the "Prime Season" is based on what has been traditionally the very best time of the year to dive a specific destination. However, it is not uncommon to get flat water, sunshine, 100 feet of visibility, etc. during the "off season". We are just attempting to inform the reader of traditional climatic conditions for each specific destination.

Note: Divers must realize that scheduling your trip during the "Prime Season" is in no way a guarantee you will not have a storm and in fact, for many destinations, the hurricane season is also the prime season to dive. Trade wind season brings gentle to strong prevailing winds which usually produce sunny weather. Though the winds do have a pleasant cooling effect, they can also make the water rough for diving or crossings.

Famous dive sites: Listed here are many world famous dive sites. This category is for those of you who have heard of a site, but didn't know where it was located. Keep in mind that the famous sites, are not necessarily *still* the best ones.

Live Aboards: The vessels mentioned have been in Business for at least a few years and have established a good reputation at the time of printing. **Note:** *This category does not represent ALL of the Live-Aboards found in each destination. For more detailed information on individual vessels refer to "Live-Aboards of the World" Vol. I and "Asian Diver Asia - Pacific Live-Aboards."*

Most feature, or even surpass the following standards:

- Air conditioned staterooms
- Air conditioned salon
- E 6 processing
- Spacious dive deck
- Large quantities of fresh (hot) water
- Charging stations
- Quality food service

Since operators come and go, it's impossible to be assured of the quality of each operator's vessel and business standard. We recommend you refer back to "Live-Aboard Selection" and inspect each vessel's brochure for amenities, size, passenger-crew ratio, etc. Study the "How to check up on information you received" section in the chapter *"Booking your trip"* to evaluate the operator's reputation.

Additional Comments: Comments and tips from the authors, professional tour leaders and others who are experts on the particular destination, meaning that they have been there many times over several years.

Bahamas

Overview: The Bahamas are made up of over 700 flat limestone islands and countless islets and cays scattered in a long chain over 100,000 square miles. Many of the remote outer islands are still pristine and unexplored. Nassau and Freeport offer additional attractions such as duty free shopping and casinos.

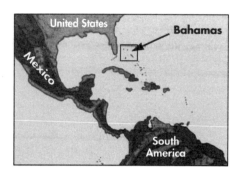

Location: The chain of the Bahamas begins 50 miles east of Fort Lauderdale, Florida, and stretches 600 miles southeastward.

Airlines: Air Canada, American, Carnival Airlines, Delta, Bahamas Air.

Airport: Nassau and Freeport International Airport. Many Live-Aboards leave from Miami and Fort Lauderdale.

Documents: US and Canadian citizens need proof of ID, such as a birth certificate and a returning or on going airline ticket. All other nationalities need valid passport.

Climate: Winter daytime temperatures are in the 70's, chilling off into the 60's at night. Summer time temperatures can be in the low 90's. Hurricane season is from July to October.

Visibility: Averages at 100 ft in summer. During winter storms visibility can be cut down to less than 50 ft.

Currents: Weak to non existent in most areas. Stronger in channels and some wall dives.

Water temperature: Low 70's in winter, 80's in summer.

Crossings: Very rough during winter months, specially in the northern islands. Calm during summer months, except when hurricanes occur in the area.

Water Condition: Flat during summer months, except when hurricanes occur in the area. November through March can bring storms and rough conditions, often making it impossible to visit the area where wild dolphins are encountered.

Diving topography: Shallow reefs, sheer deep walls, caves, submarine pinnacles, blue holes and ocean holes near Andros island. The dolphins frequent an area with miles of white sandy bottom in 20 ft. water. Nearby is a wreck where loggerhead turtles, barracudas and nursesharks can be seen.

Reef structure: Numerous hard corals, such as elkhorn and staghorn coral. Some areas feature tubesponges, deep water gorgonians and black coral.

Marine life: The Bahamas are known for possible wild dolphin encounters and shark dives with shark feedings. Nassau groupers, sting rays and barracudas are also common.

Night diving: Dive sites in protected areas are generally available. Night diving features colorful macro life, sleeping parrotfish and some crustaceans.

Prime diving season: Summer, except when hurricanes occur. June is considered prime month, since winter storms are over, water temperature is increasing but hurricanes are not likely.

Famous dive site: Wild dolphin encounters (Snorkeling and free diving).

Live-Aboards: MV Ballymena, Bottom Time II

Additional Comments:

Jim Watt: *"If you are a serious photographer, and want to photograph the dolphins, I suggest you travel in a small group with the people, who have done it for years. I recommend the Dream Too."*

Bay Islands of Honduras

Overview: Four mountainous main islands and sixty small cays at the base of the world's second largest barrier reef. The mainland of Honduras offers unique opportunities to explore some of the Mayan culture.

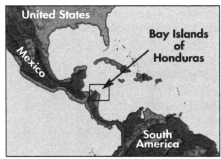

Location: 30 miles off the mainland of Honduras, Central America, and 780 miles from Miami.

Airlines: Continental, American Airlines (to the international airport on the mainland of Honduras) Lacsa, Taca.

Airport: Toncontin at the capital of Honduras, Tegucigalpa, or San Pedro Sula. From there you connect to Roatan, the largest of the Bay Islands.

Documents: All nationalities require passport and visa. If unable to obtain visa, it may be issued upon airport arrival. Return or on-going airline ticket is required.

Climate: Tropical, mostly sunny year around. Temperatures average at 75^0 F - 90^0 F. Tradewinds provide cooling effect.

Visibility: 45 - 70 ft.

Water temperature: 75^0 F in winter to 83^0 F in summer.

Crossings: Inter-island crossings take up to three hours. You are subject to open ocean conditions and the swells are variable.

Water condition: Calm to moderate on anchorages and dive sites.

Currents: Generally weak to non existent, but occasionally, moderate currents can be experienced at some of the dive sites.

Diving topography: Shallow reefs, beginning at 20 - 25 ft. and drop off to about 80 ft. Then, they extend very gradually toward the bottom. Overall the good diving is shallow, including off shore seamounts, tunnels, caves and over hangs.

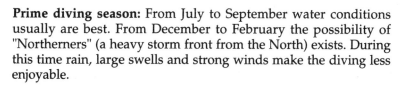

Reef structure: Gorgonians, encrusting sponges, sea whips, black coral, huge barrel and elephant ear sponges.

Marine life highlights: Fabulous macro photography, such as seahorses, tunicates and frogfish. Encounters with blue water pelagics when diving the seamounts.

Night diving: Can be done very shallow. Good and very colorful macro life.

Prime diving season: From July to September water conditions usually are best. From December to February the possibility of "Northerners" (a heavy storm front from the North) exists. During this time rain, large swells and strong winds make the diving less enjoyable.

Famous dive site: Toontown.

Live-Aboards: Bay Island Aggressor, Wind Dancer.

Belize Islands

Overview: More than 200 cays and three atolls scattered off the mainland of Belize, sheltered by the world's second largest barrier reef. You are unlikely to encounter any day charter boats. There is a bird sanctuary on Half Moon Cay at the Light House Atoll. Live-

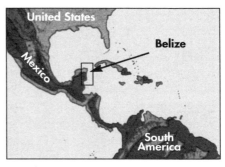

Aboards can arrange for visits. The mainland of Belize features many archaeological sites to explore the Mayan culture as well as the only jaguar preserve in the world.

Location: 100 miles south of Cozumel, Mexico, 425 miles south of Miami, in Central America.

Airlines: Continental, Taca, American, Sahsa.

Airport: Philip S.W. Goldson International Airport, Belize City.

Documents: Valid passport, return or on-going airline ticket. Visas are not required for citizens of the United States, Canada, Mexico, United Kingdom, most other European countries.

Climate: Sub-tropical with cooling constant trade winds. The annual air temperatures average between 75⁰ - 90⁰ F. Between March and October you'll find tradewinds to be strongest. January through April are hot and dry. June through September is the rainy season.

Visibility: Often exceeding 100 feet in late spring and summer, but rough seas and a heavy concentration of plankton can sometimes limit the visibility to 50 feet or less. The visibility also tends to vary with the tides, outgoing tides can temporarily cut the viz to 30 feet.

Water temperatures: Down to 75⁰ F in winter, up to 85⁰ F in summer.

Crossings: Expect a four hour crossing from Belize City to Lighthouse reef on the evening of arrival.

Water condition: Generally very calm. But since the islands are flat, they provide little to no shelter from any approaching storms. So, if the weather turns, conditions will result in swells and wind chops on the dive sites.

Currents: Mild to non existent.

Diving topography: Most of the best diving takes place off three main atolls located outside of the barrier reef. You will find vertical walls, that start as shallow as 25 feet and drop off into the abyss. Tunnels and caves. Shallow sandy outcroppings where you can look for sting rays and nurse sharks.

Reef structure: Elephant ear and barrel sponges, gorgonian sea fans. Wide array of hard corals.

Marine life highlights: Mantas, barracudas, turtles, stingrays, large groupers, and colorful tropicals, including beautiful large angelfish and good macro life, such as arrow crabs.

Night diving: Nocturnal Caribbean octopus, sleeping parrot fish, good macro. Easy night diving.

Prime diving season:
March through May.

Famous dive sites:
The Blue Hole.

Live-Aboards: Wave Dancer,
Belize Aggressor.

Additional Comments:
"The country side in Belize is very beautiful, but avoid any unnecessary layover time in Belize City, due to the high crime rate. Don't go out alone, always travel in large groups."

"Don't miss the Booby bird sanctuary on Half Moon Key"
The Authors

Cayman Islands

Overview: The Caymans are made up of three flat limestone islands that are located at the top of a sea mount that plunges thousands of feet into the abyss. Grand Cayman is twenty two miles long, eleven miles wide and is well developed with several hotels, restaurants, duty free shops and dive operators. Cayman Brac and Little Cayman are much smaller and less developed.

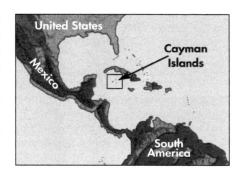

Location: 495 miles south of Miami.

Airlines: Cayman Airways, American, Northwest.

Airport: Owen Roberts International (Grand Cayman) Edward Bodden Airport (Little Cayman).

Climate: Mostly sunny. 80^0 F - 90^0 F in summer, 70^0 F - 80^0 F in winter. Rainy season is from October till March.

Visibility: 70 - 150 feet.

Water temperature: 78^0 F- 82^0 F.

Crossings: Open ocean conditions exist during inter-island crossing. Crossings can be rough, and, weather permitting, are sometimes considered impossible.

Water condition: When the weather is good, which often is the case, the water can be glassy calm and the visibility spectacular. But, since the flat Cayman Islands don't offer much for protection, anchorages can be rough, when storms or hurricanes do approach.

Currents: Currents are usually weak to non existent.

Diving topography: Vertical walls, honeycombed tunnels and caverns, shallow coral reefs and a few wrecks.

Reef structure: Seafans, huge elephant ear and barrel sponges and stunningly beautiful red sponges. (Remember you have to shine your light on them to see the color. Otherwise they appear like black/brown lumps on the reef and are easily ignored).

Marine life highlights: Schools of shimmering tarpon, turtles, stingrays, eagle rays and tame fish. Very impressively sized and colored angelfish: French Angel, Queen Angel, Gray Angelfish, all very friendly and easy to photograph. Molly the manta at Little Cayman.

Night diving: Abundant sleeping parrot fish, lots of macro life, easy night diving.

Prime diving season: May through November is considered prime season, except when hurricanes pass through (Summer is hurricane season). May and June tend to promise most stable conditions, as northern storms are unlikely and hurricane season has not yet arrived. During the December to March period storms are possible.

Famous dive site: Sting Ray City, Babalon, and Bloody Bay Wall (Little Cayman).

Live-Aboards: Cayman Aggressor II, Little Cayman Diver.

Additional Comments:
"The Caymans offer some of the easiest and best diving in the Carribbean. Though over-developed on the west side of Grand Cayman, Live-Aboards offer Cayman dive sites that day boats cannot access."

"Excellent location to learn underwater photography"
The Authors

Turks & Caicos, Carribbean

Overview: The island group consists of eight arid limestone islands and more than thirty cays. The northern shore of the island of Provo is a marine preserve.

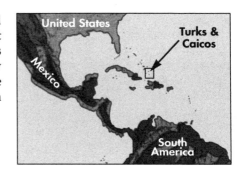

Location: 575 miles southeast of Miami, 30 miles south of the Bahamas.

Airlines: American, Cayman Airways, Turks and Caicos Airlines, Carnival Airlines.

Airport: Provo.

Documents: US and Canadian citizens need proof of identity. All other nationalities need a passport.

Climate: Dry, with little rainfall and near constant winds. Summer temperatures range up to 95° F, winter temperatures rarely lower than 75° F.

Visibility: 80 - 150 ft in deeper water. Visibility on shallow reefs sometimes restricted.

Water temperature: 72° F - 78° F winter, 80° F - 82° F summer.

Diving topography: Deep vertical walls, generally starting at about 40 - 50 ft. Ledges and grottoes.

Reef structure: Hardcorals, such as elkhorn, brain and plate corals. Huge barrel, elephant ear and tube sponges.

Marine life highlights: Lots of big fish, rays, turtles and migrating humpbacks during the winter months. Jojo the tame dolphin.

Night diving: Excellent colorful sponges and macro life.

Prime diving season: April through September, except when hurricanes pass through. The winter months are occasionally accompanied by rainstorms, but on the good side, this is the season for migrating humpbacks to frequent the area.

Famous dive site: North West Point.

Live-Aboards: Peter Hughes' Sea Dancer, Turks and Caicos Aggressor.

Coco Island, Costa Rica

Overview: Uninhabited, rainforest covered island, with spectacular waterfalls and a vivid history of piracy. You may encounter another Live-Aboard but due to the distance to the mainland no day charter boats. There are thirty National Parks on the mainland of 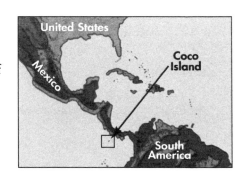 Costa Rica, including deserted beaches, active volcanoes and pristine rainforest.

Location: 360 miles off the west coast of Costa Rica.

Airlines: Lacsa Airlines, Aviateca, American, Continental, TACA, United.

Airports: San Jose International Airport.

Documents: US citizens may enter with proof of citizenship plus photo ID and tourist card, but a valid passport is recommended. All other nationalities must have a passport and return or on going ticket.

Climate: Rainfall is common year around. June through August tend to be even wetter. Average temperatures 78 - 85 degrees.

Visibility: 30-100 feet. You will find visibility drop when entering thermoclines.

Water temperature: Generally in the low 80's low 70s, with temperatures dropping into the high 60s in deep thermoclines zones.

Crossings: A 34 - 40 hour crossing is necessary to reach Coco Island from the mainland of Costa Rica. You'll be crossing open ocean, and even with very good water and weather conditions, the crossing is still considered rough by most divers. The fact that everything (TV, deck chairs, etc.) on the boats is permanently bolted and tied down, should be a hint.

Water condition: The surface around the dive sites is often rough, with large swells and whitecaps. It rains regularly, limiting the visibility at the surface even more. Bright colors and safety sausages are a must. There are a few protected bays, where the mothership finds safe and calm anchorage.

Currents: The currents can be very strong (But the stronger the current, the more shark action), and can easily take you miles off the dive site, if you don't watch out.

Diving topography: Mostly rocky terrain, sand at the bottom of the walls.

Reef structure: Some encrusting sponges, very little hard coral.

Marine life highlights: Schooling hammerhead sharks, jacks and tuna. Large manta rays, whalesharks, marbled sting rays and other pelagics. Interesting macro life, too, but often overlooked.

Night diving: Although night diving is possible at sites without currents, night dives are not a major attraction mostly due to the thousand of spiny sea urchins, which clutter the bottom. Common to see *many* active whitetip reef sharks.

Prime diving season: November to May. October is considered the worst month with rougher conditions and stronger currents.

Famous dive site: Dirty rock, Manuelita.

Live-Aboards: Okeanos Aggressor, Undersea Hunter, Sea Hunter.

Additional Comments:

"Cocos offers some of the best pelagic diving in the world, but don't go there looking for a suntan"

"Bring shoes to hike to the water-falls during surface intervals"

"Arrive a few days before the boat departs so that any lost luggage can catch up with you. Once the boat leaves port, you will not be able to get any bags"

The Authors

"Just as sharks are finally beginning to get some recognition as a vital component of the ecosystem, and one of the most exciting experiences you can ever have underwater, many populations are simultaneously coming under threat of extinction due to uncontrolled commercial fishing, often utilizing only the fins. Coco Island is one of the few places where you can still see awesome schools of hundred of hammerheads, as well as whitetips, Galapagos sharks, silky sharks, whalesharks, mantas, dolphins, turtles etc."

Doug Perrine

Galapagos

Overview: Thirteen volcanic islands and numerous smaller islets, all part of the Galapagos national park, which only permits 40,000 visitors per year. Land visits are offered by all Live-Aboard operators and feature Galapagos sea lions, flamingos, tortoises and iguanas.

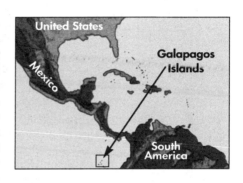

Location: 600 miles west of Ecuador on the equator.

Airlines: Saeta, American.

Airport: International Airport in Quito or Guayaquil, Ecuador. From there you fly into San Christobal, Galapagos Islands. Watch out for tight luggage restrictions between Quito and Galapagos.

Documents: Valid passport by all nationalities. No visa is required by Canadian and US citizens.

Climate: The temperature remains close to the same year around. August and September tend to be overcast, but dry and windy. January till April is the rainy, but warmer season.

Visibility: Ranges between 40 and 80 feet, but can change drastictly from one dive to the next, sometimes even within the same dive.

Currents: Very strong and unpredictable. Can change rapidly and without warning during a dive. Currents can go up, down, whirlpool and move in both directions horizontally all in one dive.

113

Water temperature: Generally ranges from high 50's to low 80's. Both temperature extremes can be experienced in one dive. Thermoclines can be layers of cold water at the surface as well as at depth or even occur perpendicular. Due to the phenomena it's possible to see tropical fish and penguins, all in one dive. August and September tend to be the months with the coldest temperatures. During an "El Nino" current water temperatures can rise into the 80's, but abundance of large pelagics may decrease, or are found in much deeper and colder water.

Crossings: A minimum of a sixteen hours crossing is necessary to get to the northern islands, Wolf and Darwin. This is where some of the best diving and pelagic encounters are experienced. Generally, crossings in the Galapagos are surprisingly calm, with only occasional rough water conditions.

Water condition: Generally the motherships find shelter at protected bays for calm nightly anchorages, but dive sites can be choppy, usually due to the strong currents. Again, this will vary with the weather, but prepare for rougher conditions, especially during August and September.

Diving topography: Rocky with little coral. Three main currents feed this area which brings both planktonic young and adult marine life.

Reef structure: Some hardcoral, patches of tubastrea coral, black coral.

Marine life highlights: Schools of hammerheads, dolphins, turtles, eagle rays, moray eels fur seals, massive schools of fish, butterfly fish, manta rays, iguanas, penguins, red lipped batfish, golden-red seahorses, as well as the occasional encounter with whale sharks, Galapagos sharks, killer whales. Marine life varies from island to island as well as with currents.

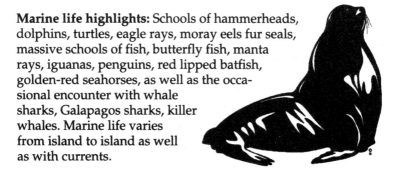

Night diving: Possible in some areas with protected coves. Night dives give you an opportunity to observe macro life such as seahorses and batfish, often overlooked during the day due to encounters with large fish.

Prime diving season: December to May are considered the best months, since generally the currents are less severe, the seas calmer and the water tends to be warmer and clearer.

Famous dive site: Roca Redonda.

Live-Aboards: Galapagos Aggressor I and II, Reina Silvia, Lammerlaw.

Additional Comments:

"The photographic opportunities are endless.
Bring twice as much film as you think you will need!"
                                                                Mark Bernardi

"When travelling independently in Ecuador before your Live-Aboard charter, I recommend that you arrange for a representative of the company you're diving with to meet you at the airport anyway. The custom procedures at the international airport can be very bothersome for photographers. On your layover in Ecuador choose Quito rather than Guayaquil. Quito is in a beautiful, clean location in the mountains, while Guayaquil is a polluted coastal city."
                                                                Jim Watt

Kona Coast / Island of Hawaii

Overview: Kona is actually the name of a district located on the western (leeward) side of the Big Island of Hawaii. Volcanic in nature, the Big Island offers some of the most diverse climatic conditions in the world. From snow capped peaks, tropical rainforest to lava deserts, a drive around the island is similar to a quick trip around the world.

Kauai

Oahu

Maui

Kona Coast

Big Island

HAWAIIAN ISLANDS

Location: 30 minutes southeast of Honolulu, approximately 2500 miles west of the mainland USA.

Airlines: Hawaiian, United, American, Continental and most other major carriers.

Airport: Keahole Airport.

Documents: For US citizens no documents required.

Climate: Day time temperatures range from mid 70's to mid 80's. Winter can get fairly cool at night (mid 60's). The summer months tend to be wetter and hurricanes can occur.

Visibility: 80 - 150 feet. Usually Kona's visibility is excellent. With no agricultural run off and the absence of large sandy beaches, only large open ocean swells or the occasional hurricanes in summer, reduce visibility.

Water temperature: May to October: 78 - 82° F, November to April: 72 - 76° F.

Crossings: No inter-island crossing. Can get rough for short runs through areas exposed to tradewinds.

Water condition: Most of the coast is exposed to open ocean swells with only a few truly protected anchorages to hide from unexpected weather. Fortunately, the prevailing weather patterns bring calm to moderate swell conditions. Since Kona is located on the leeward side of this high volcanic island, it has very little exposure to prevailing tradewinds.

Diving topography: Sloping walls, volcanic formations such as lava tubes, caverns, arches and hard coral gardens.

Reef structure: Varied types of hard coral, such as cauliflower coral, endemic finger coral and antlercoral. Patches of tubastrea coral, leather coral (octo coral) and black coral on a few "secret" deep dives. Encrusting sponges in all possible colors.

Marine life highlights: A great variety of crustaceans, endemic fish species, humpback whales from late December to early April. Usually seen at the surface. Frogfish, manta rays, friendly turtles and the occasional whale shark, eagle ray or even monk seal.

Night diving: Excellent and easy. Five species of lobsters, anemone crabs, spanish dancers, nocturnal octopus and much more.

Prime diving season: July through November has the flattest water and the best visibility, but since it's hurricane season, hurricanes, though rare in Hawaii, are possible. January till March the water conditions can be rough (but aren't always) due to Northwest swells. The water temperatures also drop to the lower seventies. But since at this time humpback whales mate and give birth in Hawaiian waters, the trade off may be worth it.

Famous dive site: Manta Ray Village.

Live Aboards: Kona Aggressor II.

Additional comments:

"Bring a hood and a full wet suit, even in summer, if you plan to do five dives a day and have a tendency to get chilled easily. Great place to learn photography. Since the diving is relatively easy, you can concentrate on your camera equipment, develop your eye on spotting macro life and learn about endemic fish species!"

"During whaleseason bring a land camera with a telephoto lens for spectacular whale photography opportunities"

The Authors

Fiji Islands

Overview: 322 islands offer varied topography, from mountainous islands to flat sandy atolls.

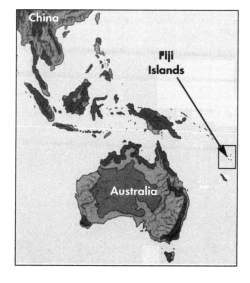

Location: 5200 miles southwest of Los Angeles, 1100 miles north of New Zealand.

Airlines: Air New Zealand, Air Pacific.

Airport: Nadi International Airport.

Documents: All nationalities must have a passport, valid for at least six months beyond the intended stay in Fiji and a return or on going ticket. US, New Zealand, Australian, Canadian and Japanese citizen do not need a visa.

Climate: Tropical, tempered by trade winds. The summer's wet season is from December to March. The climate and annual rainfall vary greatly from island group to island group. We recommend that you contact the Live-Aboard you're interested in, about the proposed itinerary (may vary with season) and study the water and weather conditions in a travel guide.

Visibility: 100 feet plus at offshore reefs and islands. Due to runoffs of the main islands' rivers, the visibility is generally limited close to shore.

Currents: Although in some areas currents may be mild or absent, some of the best action dives are when and where the currents are running.

Water temperature: 80 - 84⁰ F in summer, 75 - 77⁰ F in winter.

Crossings: Inter island crossings are necessary for most itineraries. Generally it's true, that the further you travel off the main island, the better the visibility and the more abundant the marine life. As in most places crossings are subject to open ocean conditions.

Water condition: Varies greatly with regional and seasonal changes. From August till November the water tends to be flattest.

Diving topography: Sheer walls, inner lagoons, pinnacles, sloping reefs, channels.

Reef structure: Softcorals, seafans, sponges, anemones, gorgonians, crynoids.

Marine life: Varies greatly from area to area. As a rule of thumb, due to river run off and population, the further your trip takes you from the main island, the greater your chances are to see pelagics and unique creatures. Macro life is vivid and plentiful throughout the island chain.

Night diving: Generally done in calm bays, featuring macro life such as decorator crabs, shrimps and fish in their dormant state.

Prime diving season: April to end of November, October/ November being the best time for flat water.

Live-Aboards: Nai'a, Matagi Princess, Fiji Aggressor (to be launched in 1997).

Additional Comments:

"Go for at least 10 days to dive the outer islands and see the true Fiji diving! Expect much more than just great diving. The Fijians are some of the friendliest people on the planet."

Rob Barrel

Indonesia

Overview: With over 14,000 islands this is the world's largest archipelago. Besides world class diving, Indonesia offers interesting cultural and spectacular scenic highlights, as well as a wide diversity in Flora and Fauna. Malaria is a problem in many regions in Indonesia.

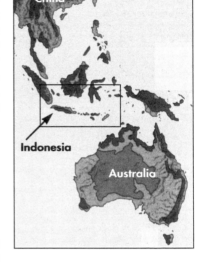

Airlines: Garuda Airlines, Malaysia Airlines, Singapore Airlines.

Airport: Jakarta.

Documents: Valid passports are required and must have at least six months left before expiration. US citizens may remain for up to 60 days without a formal visa, though you receive a dated stamp upon entry.

Climate: The climate zones in Indonesia are as varied as the islands' topography. Generally the dry season is from May to October and the rainy season from November to April. Since the area is so vast, you should inquire about the itinerary of the Live-Aboard you are considering, and then read up in travel guides about the exact topography, climate and seasonal weather occurrences.

Visibility: Varies greatly with seasonal and regional changes. During the prime weather season visibility averages 100 ft.

Currents: Currents range from mild to very strong. They can start and stop without warning and run in all directions, including up and down currents.

Water temperature: Almost constant in the 80's.

Crossings: Be prepared for potentially rough crossings. Crossings take generally at least a few hours in between islands, often longer. Inquire for details with each Live-Aboard operator. Just because crossings are not mentioned in the brochure doesn't mean, they don't do any. Ask for the proposed itinerary, or at least which area is usually dived and then look at a detailed map of Indonesia.

Water condition: Varies greatly with seasonal and regional changes. From glassy calm, to very rough. Protected bays for nightly anchorages are often available. January and February can produce very rough seas.

Diving topography: Sheer walls, slopes, mangrove, reef flat, pinnacles, active underwater volcanic vents, wrecks, caves.

Marine life: Some of the most varied marine life in the world. Marine biologists have called it "the dispersal center of all underwater species."

Night diving: Great macro life, but anything is possible. Protected bays can generally be found for night dives.

Prime diving season: Generally the water is flattest during the dry season, while January and February are frequented by rainstorms and rough seas.
The following are the prime seasons in various areas:

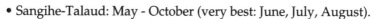

- Sangihe-Talaud: May - October (very best: June, July, August).

- Ambon: September - December.

- Banda Sea: March - June, October, November.

- Java: March - November (very best: May - September).

- Komodo (south): November - January.

- West Irian Jaya: March - November (very best: July - September).

Live-Aboards: There is no Live-Aboard at this time we have consistently heard good reports about. We recommend that you inspect the history and the political position of the Live-Aboards thoroughly before you hand out your money. But since this area offers some of the best diving in the world, with mostly unspoiled reefs, we decided to include this destination.

Additional Comments:

"Overweight baggage charges are incurred everywhere. However, Garuda Airlines, in order to encourage divers traveling to Indonesia, allows three pieces of baggage and more allowed weight, if "diver" is written when the ticket is issued. If the six months passport stipulation is violated they send you right back home at your own expense. If you over-stay your two month limit they may not allow you back. "

Mike and Pauline Severns

"Indonesia and the adjacent Philippines have the richest marine fauna and flora in the world, with possibly 3000 species of fish or more, with many of them still remaining to be described. However, the reefs are not entirely unspoilt anymore. I have seen a real diminution in the population of larger fishes since I first dived in Indonesia in the 70's. There is no question that overfishing has had a major impact on Indonesian reefs, no doubt as a result of the overpopulation of humans. Sharks have been especially hard hit, because of the high prices Taiwanese are offering for sharkfins, but it is also a real event to find a large grouper, emperor and snapper. Schools of jacks are now rare."

Jack Randall

Papua New Guinea

Overview: New Guinea combines some extremely rugged, mountainous large islands with hundreds of tiny atolls. Besides diving, it offers a vivid culture, a strong WWII history and interesting terrestrial wild life. Malaria can be a problem.

Location: South of the equator, north of Australia.

Airlines: Air Niugini, Continental, Solomon Airlines, Quantas.

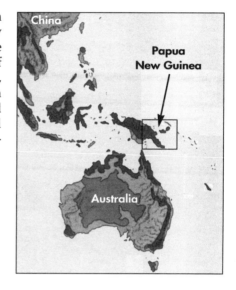

Airport: Port Moresby.

Documents: All nationalities are required to have a passport. Tourists who wish to remain in the country for more than 30 days are issued a visa, providing they have a return or on going ticket.

Climate: Tropical and hot, wet and humid. New Guinea is a large country and the geography varies greatly. Some of the mountain peaks on the larger island are 12,000 feet high. In most places the wet season is from December to March, the dry (or not so wet season) is from May to November. On the outer islands, where Live-Aboards frequent, it tends to be sunnier. But this can vary in different parts of the country, and overall, the weather in Papua New Guinea can be very unpredictable in many regions. We recommend you purchase a travel guide and study it thoroughly before you make any decisions on where and when to go.

Visibility: Averaging at 80 - 100 plus feet.

Currents: Vary with locations and tidal occurrences. From nonexistent to very strong, including up and down currents.

Water temperature: Summer (November-January) mid 80's, winter (June-August) mid to high 70's.

Crossings: Crossings are done frequently. During the months of October, November, sometimes December, crossings can be very smooth. Rest of the year crossings are generally rougher, due to swells and wind chops.

Water condition: During the prime season mostly glassy calm. Since there are many protected bays, night anchorages can be moderately calm, even if the weather picks up a little.

Diving topography: Varies from area to area. Sheer walls, submarine pinnacles, shallow reefs and lagoons.

Marine life: Located in the marinelife dispersal center of the Pacific Ocean, New Guinea offers many rare species of fish and other marine creatures. Known for frequent pelagic encounters. Killerwhales can often be seen in Kimbe Bay.

Night diving: Night diving features a wide array of macro life.

Prime diving season: April until beginning of December. Very best months for flat water are October and November. June to September can be quite windy. December to February is monsoon season. A reverse pattern can be found on the South Coast of New Britain. This area tends to be dry and calm during the months of January, February and March.

Live-Aboards: MV Febrina (Kimbe Bay, Witu Islands, New Britain) MV Telita (Milne Bay), MV Tiata (northern New Guinea), Peter Huges Star Dancer (originally Palau Sun Dancer) to be relocated in early 1997.

Additional Comments:

"Diving with dolphins in virgin, undisturbed areas. Pipefish, cuttlefish and other unique creatures."

Mark Bernardi

"Great variety of dive sites: Deep walls, deep pinnacles, shallow reefs, strong currents some places with huge seafans, no currents other places. Tons of fish. Very, very good diving. Not as many sharks as there used to be, which is getting to be a problem everyplace."

Ann Fielding

"We travel to PNG, when the general rainy season arrives in January through March. At this time, the South Coast of New Britain is typically dry and calm, which allows us to explore new and exciting dive sites."

Chris Newbert and
Birgitte Wilms

"Villagers are friendly and you may find yourself surrounded by canoes with laughing children ... The opportunity to interface with a culture that has had contact with the modern world in only the last fifty years makes this scuba diving adventure a special adventure."

Tom Campbell

The Great Barrier Reef / Coral Sea

Overview: The Great Barrier Reef is the largest reef in the world and stretches over 1500 miles along the east coast of Australia and is composed of 2900 individual reefs and more than 600 islands generally with fringing reefs. The best diving is found in the Far North and in the Coral Sea.

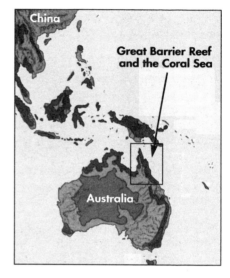

Location: The Great Barrier Reef runs along the state of Queensland in the north east region of Australia. The Coral Sea is located north-east of the Great Barrier Reef.

Airlines: Quantas.

Airport: Cairns, Townsville.

Documents: A visa is required to enter Australia by all visiting nationalities except New Zealand, as well as a passport which is valid longer than the intended stay.

Climate: Tropical, the wet season being from October till March, with temperatures in the mid 80's. The Cyclone season tends to be in February and March. The dry season (winter) from April till September brings temperatures in the 70's. June till August can be windy. September tends to be perfectly calm with very little wind.

In November the "doldrums" hit, bringing steamy hot, but very calm conditions with little wind.

Visibility: 40' - 60' ft. inside the Barrier Reef. 100' - 150' feet on outer reefs. 100' - 250' in the Far North and Coral Sea.

Currents: Currents are heaviest during full moon and usually occur in channels, not necessarily on walls. Up and down currents are possible but not common.

Water temperature: Low to mid 70's in winter months, low 80's in summer. Slightly warmer in the "Far North" and Coral Sea.

Crossings: Crossings take many hours, especially to reach the remote areas, where diving is best. Due to lack of protective mountainous islands crossings can be very rough if wind or storm conditions are present. September through November are generally the months with the flattest water and most comfortable for long crossings.

Water Condition: Water condition at dive sites is generally calm. The reefs provide great shelters even in rougher condition. Safe and calm nightly anchorages are always available in lagoons or leeside of the reefs.

Diving topography: Extreme drop-offs, submerged bommies, shipwrecks, shallow lagoons, pinnacles.

Reef structure: Staghorn coral and other hardcorals. Soft corals, gorgonian fans, anemones, even more so in outer Coral Sea.

Marine life: Giant potato groupers and napoleon wrasses, tiger-sharks, reef sharks, wobbegong sharks, giant clams, large schools of reef fish, turtles. Macro life is plentiful and sometimes rare species are found. Marine life tends to be more abundant and untouched on the remote reefs of the Far North and Coral Sea.

Night diving: Calm spots without currents are always available. Excellent shell life, crustaceans, sleeping fish, flashlight fish.

129

Prime diving season: September through January. Very best September through November. During February to April, swells can be large and overall conditions rough, and diving in the remote Coral Sea is generally not done.

Famous dive site: Cod hole, S.S. Yongala (wreckdive), Northhorn in Osprey Reef.

Live-Aboards: Reef Explorer, Undersea Explorer, Spoil Sport.

Additional Comments:

"I have seen some of the best visibility, largest soft coral trees and frequency of shark encounters in the Coral Sea."

Jim Watt

Solomon Islands

Overview: With over 900 mountainous islands, atolls and cays the Solomons are the third largest archipelago in the world. Since the Solomon Islands are scattered over more than a 1000 miles, the chances of meeting one of the few Live-Aboards or day charter boats are virtually zero. The Solomons offer unique opportunities for cultural experiences and a strong WWII history.

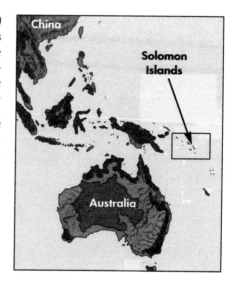

Location: Between 7 and 12 degrees south of the equator, 1250 miles northeast across the Coral Sea from Queensland, Australia.

Airlines: Solomon Airlines. (Route through Nadi, Fiji Brisbane, Australia or Auckland, New Zealand with Air New Zealand or Quantas, and Air Pacific) Air Niguini: once a week from Port Moresby to Honiara and back.

Airport: Henderson Field. Located ten minutes from Honiara, the capital.

Documents: Citizens of British Commonwealth, US and most EEC do not require a visa but most hold a passport and a return or on going ticket to enter the country.

Climate: Tropical, humid and hot, but moderated by the cooling effect of trade winds. Annual daytime temperatures average at 85⁰ F. April until November is considered dry season. December to April is the monsoon season, during which hurricanes may form.

Visibility: 60 - 150 ft. Rarely affected by weather conditions, because of the many protected dive sites, but plankton accumulation can lower visibility at times.

Currents: Although there are many dive sites in protected bays with no currents present, most of the wall dives are frequented by mild to very strong currents, including, at times, up and down currents.

Water temperature: 78⁰ F in winter (July), 86⁰ F in summer (December), averaging at 82⁰ F to 84⁰ F throughout the year.

Crossings: Inter-island crossings are necessary to commute between island groups. Some crossings can take up to seven hours, but are usually done at night. Crossings can be rough! Six to eight foot swells are not uncommon. Other times the sea presents herself so calm, you hardly know you are underway.

Water condition: Night anchorages and dive site are usually quite calm.

Diving topography: Varies from island group to island group. Sloping walls, sheer drop offs, submarine pinnacles, caves and caverns, some WWII wrecks.

Reef structure: Softcorals, black coral, some sponges, seafans, gorgonians, hardcorals, anemones.

Marine life: Rare macro life, wide array of tropicals, sharks, manta rays, eagle rays, schooling batfish and barracudas, occasionally whales and crocodiles. Almost anything is possible.

Night diving: Many species of decorator crabs, flashlight fish, rare shrimp and much more. Some areas are exposed to currents, be prepared.

Prime diving season: Mid September - December. Although still considered cyclone season, March and April can also be excellent. Cyclones usually form in the Solomons, and are exported into other areas south. Due to numerous protected bays, even if a cyclone hits the area, you will most likely be able to continue diving as normal, although crossings may get rough! May till October trade winds are blowing, making for rough crossings, and surface chop, but visibility usually remains good.

Famous dive site: Barracuda point.

Live-Aboards: Bilikiki, Spirit of Solomons and Solomon Sea.

Additional Comments:

"Hundreds of WWII wrecks lie in the waters of the Solomon Islands. However, most of them are thousands of feet deep. There are a few shallower ones, but since most of them are in lagoons with extremely limited visibility and/or are a long distance from quality reefs and/or are in fairly poor condition, it is questionable if they are worth visiting. Visit the Solomons for the reefs, marine life and cultural highlights, go to Truk Lagoon for the wrecks!"

"Solomon Airlines' luggage restrictions are limited to 66 lbs. Pack accordingly."

The Authors

"The Solomons is one of the richest, most diverse coral reef environments on earth. It remains virtually untouched in the truest sense of the word."

Chris Newbert

Palau (Belau), Micronesia

Overview: The archipelago consists of some 340 islands stretched out over 400 miles. Only eight of these islands are inhabited with the main island of Babeldob rising to over 700 feet. Palau is surrounded by a barrier reef and teeming with marinelife. Once a little known dive spot in the Pacific, Palau has recently gained much notoriety as a top dive destination. There are now several more dive operators and charter boats competing for dive sites with the increased number of Live-Aboards.

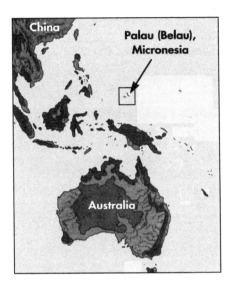

Location: East of the Philippines and seven degrees (400 miles) north of the equator.

Airlines: Continental Air Micronesia, Air Nairu.

Airport: Palau International Airport, near the capital, Koror.

Documents: US citizens are required to hold a passport, certified birth certificate or voter's registration card. Other nationalities need to have a passport.

Climate: Tropical, hot and humid. The average temperature is 81°F, but during the rainy season from June to August, the water temperature, at times, appears to be warmer than the air. Bring appropriate clothing. Overall the weather is fairly unpredictable, with sunny and rainy days taking turns. Driest season is from February and April.

Visibility: Averages 60 feet inside lagoons, 100 plus feet on outer reefs. Affected by tidal changes.

Water temperatures: 80 - 86°F.

Crossings: Crossings are short and occur mainly inside barrier reef and calm lagoons.

Water condition: Palau tends to be windy. Common to experience moderate to strong wind chop.

Currents: Moderate to very very strong, including up and down currents, on the outer reefs and in the channels. Dives in protected bays seldom experience currents.

Diving topography: Sheer vertical walls on outer reefs, channel drifts, inner reefs, salt water marine lake, blue holes, caverns, mangrooves and a few WWII wrecks.

Reef structure: Softcoral, gorgonians, anemones, whip corals, hardcorals.

Marine life highlights: Sharks, barracudas, turtles, lionfish, nautilus (if trapped), giant clams, 1500 species of fish. Manta ray cleaning stations.

Night diving: Night diving possible in protected lagoons. Excellent macro life.

Prime diving season: December through April.

Famous dive sites: Blue Corner, Jellyfish lake, Ngemelis Dropoff and Big Dropoff.

135

Live-Aboards: Peter Hughes' Sun Dancer II, Palau Aggressor II.

Additional Comments:

"One special dive is Jellyfish lake (non stinging jellyfish). This is a snorkel dive, and you have to walk over some rough, possibly muddy terrain to reach the lake. Therefore: bring some walking shoes, sunhat and some gloves. Some of the plants are toxic (make you itch), so the gloves keep the itchy stuff off your body."

Jim Church

"If you are looking for more adventurous, less structured diving in Palau, try the smaller Live-Aboard Oceanhunter."

Jim Watt

Truk Lagoon (Chuuk), Micronesia

Overview: Encircled by over 140 miles of protective barrier reef, Truk Lagoon is home to over sixty sunken WWII ships, planes, submarines and other war artifacts. Often considered the "Disney-land" of ship wreck diving, these Japanese wrecks can be found at various depths. Though most of the small artifacts have been removed from the wrecks, the ships now boast some of the most spectacular coral growth in the world.

Location: Truk Lagoon is located seven degrees north of the equator, 650 miles southeast of Guam, 750 miles north of Papua New Guinea, 6000 miles southwest of Los Angeles .

Airlines: Continental Micronesia Airlines.

Airport: Moen Island.

Documents: Passports and visas are not required for US citizens, but must have proof of citizenship, such as birth certificate. Citizens of other countries must have a valid passport and a return or on going airline ticket. Persons visiting Truk Lagoon for more than 30 days, must obtain a visa before arrival.

137

Climate: Hot and humid. Heavy year around rainfall. Average annual temperature: 80 - 81° F. February to April are the driest months.

Visibility: Averages 50 - 80 feet. Variables are often based on where in the lagoon you are diving and the amount of plankton found. Silting is a problem when diving inside or close to the deck of the wrecks.

Water temperature: 80-84 degrees.

Crossings: Not necessary on most trips.

Water condition: Since you are in a protected lagoon, ocean swells are only felt if you go outside the barrier reef. The inside conditions go from glassy calm to a 4-6 foot wind swell if a storm approaches. Generally the lagoon is moderately calm.

Diving topography: Although there is over 140 miles of barrier reef in Truk, most of the diving is on the more than sixty shipwrecks, planes and submarines.

Reef structure: The sunken wrecks are covered with an immense growth of soft corals and anemones. The outer reefs are made up of mostly hard coral formations with some gorgonians found in the deeper depths.

Marine life: Great macro life, lionfish, clown fish and sharks on outer reefs.

Night diving: Easy and colorful. Feeding Lionfish, crabs and other nocturnal critters.

Prime diving season: December thru April. August through November tend to bring increased rainfall and chances of typhoons.

Live-Aboards: Truk Aggressor II, Thorfinn.

Additional Comments:

"Though most divers perceive Truk Lagoon as "only shipwreck diving" when in fact some of the worlds most spectacular soft coral growth can be found on these wrecks. Each ship is an ecosystem that supports itself."

The Authors

"You don't have to dive deep, and there will be much more than the wrecks. When a full-sized ship sits in 120 ft. of water, the tops of the masts are just below the surface; you don't need to visit the keel. Most important, the fish and coral life living and growing on the wrecks are fantastic!"

Jim Church

Booking Your Trip

One of the most common questions asked by divers when planning a dive adventure is "Who should I book with?" This chapter is intended to provide you with the insight to make an informed decision on which booking procedure will work best for you. You will find there are a variety of options to consider. They include:

- General travel agents
- Dive travel specialist travel agents
- Dive shops
- Direct bookings
- Escorted tour with a professional dive tour leader

When inquiring about a particular vessel, always ask for a brochure of the boat, as well as a detailed schematic of the boat's layout and if available, a video. Many times you may have to combine the services of more than one of these booking options to complete your travel plans. In the following pages, we will address the issues of booking by each of these options.

General Travel Agents

Once you've decided on a destination or are looking for more information on a specific area, booking your trip can be as easy as picking up a phone and calling an 800 number, or inquiring with your local travel agent about the desired destination. These agents are wired into the travel industries main reservation system via computer, and in theory, can handle all aspects of your travel. But, beware, SCUBA travel is a small part of the travel industry and Live-Aboards are an even smaller part.

Booking a trip to an exotic destination, thousands of miles from home, based solely on the word of a travel agent, who has never been there, let alone is unfamiliar with SCUBA diving, can be a risky proposition.

For the most part, they are simply passing along information that they are reading from a fact sheet, which is usually the companies' brochure. Sometimes they relay comments from past customers or what other agents have told them. Booking connections, including lay overs, to remote islands in the South Pacific, often requires familiarity with the specific region. If it's a popular destination that the agent has personally been to or booked several times, you should have no troubles. But unfortunately, we have often seen travelers upset and disappointed with accommodations and travel itinerary, due to misinformation by the uninformed agent.

Dive Travel Specialists

These agencies specialize in booking dive travel and are usually much more up-to-date on dive facilities in remote destinations than general travel agents. They usually will want to handle all aspects of your trip, including airfare and hotel stays along with the boat charter. As with all travel agents, their income is based on commissions where the agency receives 10 - 30% on the cost of the trip from the Live-Aboard you book. In turn, they advertise and provide a link to the public for many boat operations who are located overseas.

Realize that some agencies have the exclusive booking rights to certain vessels and receive higher commissions, when booking those vessels over the other ones. Although most of these services are very professional, be cautious of the agent who is quick to suggest another destination or vessel over the one you inquired about. Although there could be a very good legitimate reason for it, they may simply be trying to push a different destination and/or Live-Aboard because they receive a better commission.

Over the years, we have heard complaints by divers who were "scared" off a destination by "Brand X travel specialist," who said the diving in a requested destination, would be poor at the requested time, and that they would be better off going to another destination and another boat, one which of course, "Brand X travel specialist" could also book for them. Now, it is very possible the agent is telling the truth and actually giving good advise. But, it is always a good idea to get a few other opinions on why your requested destination or Live-Aboard is not available or wouldn't be suitable.

Evaluate the information you received

Many times travel agents will set the traveler up for unrealistic expectations. This often leads to misunderstandings when the diver arrives in their far away destination. Agents who promise a specific detailed day to day itinerary, obviously have spent very little time on a Live-Aboard. Sure, when you're in the travel agent's office or have your " information package" sent to you by mail, a detailed itinerary looks very professional. Unfortunately the ocean and detailed itineraries rarely agree with each other. When the wind decides to blow twenty knots and the seas are peaking at twelve feet, your trip to Little Cayman from Grand Cayman, your travel agent guaranteed you would be Monday night..., just got switched to Tuesday night ... **weather permitting** ... and, may be canceled altogether, due to an unexpected storm. Veteran divers have come to the realization that all promises made are subject to two words: "Weather permitting." When on the ocean, you base your schedule and activities around *"Mother Nature."* She is the deciding factor.

142

Travel agents who take a realistic approach may supply you with a *sample* schedule or *overview* that will give you a rough idea of activities and the type of route the vessel may take, pointing out, that changes can occur, based on the season and weather conditions.

For truly accurate information, ask to speak to an agent who has *actually* been to the destination, preferably at the time of year you are interested in. Don't take it for granted that the agent you are speaking with, has actually been to the destination, or that they have ever been on a Live-Aboard. It is possible they are not even a SCUBA diver. Don't be shy. Inquire right away if they really are an *"expert"* on this destination and if they will supply you with accurate up-to-date preparation information and support material. Remember, you will be spending thousands of dollars and traveling thousands of miles to dive. It is important that you are properly prepared for the type of diving and traveling for that region. If complications arise due to misinformation, you will be stuck to sort it out on your own. **There will be no travel agents with you to solve the problems.**

Direct Bookings

When you book directly you eliminate the middleman, lessening the risk of misinformation and promises that can't be kept. Unfortunately it can sometimes be impossible to communicate with many Live-Aboards due to the remoteness of their destination. To combat this weakness in the booking process, many operations have hired their own representative who only books them, and can be accessed via a toll free number. Some of the larger corporate and/or franchised vessels have their own inhouse travel agencies and can handle all of your travel plans, acting essentially as travel agencies.

The smaller companies will often refer you to a separate travel agency to book airfare and any hotel stays if required. It is not uncommon for a general travel agent to call these representatives and obtain air routes and more specifics to complete the booking.

Often, the representative of the operation has been to the destination and is very familiar with the details of the boat. We have found that when you book directly, you generally receive the most up-to-date information and avoid the miscommunications that often take place with many busy travel agents who have to stay informed about many areas and boats. When available, we recommend this route.

Booking through your local dive shop

Another approach to book your Live-Aboard dive trip would be through your local dive shop. But again, you run the risk of receiving poor, out-of-date information, unless they have someone who has actually been to the location aboard the specific vessel they are booking. Some dive shops are very active in the dive travel aspect of this industry, while most shops focus on local dive training and local dive trips. One criteria to look for when a shop is arranging a trip to an exotic destination is: Will there be a group leader? If so, what special talents and/or knowledge do they lend to this particular trip (i.e. photo expertise, teaching of specialty courses, local knowledge, entertainment of the group, etc...) Experienced tour leaders can turn a good trip into a fabulous one through a variety of talents and knowledge. See *Dive Travel Escorts.*

Dive Travel Escorts/ Tour Leaders

A true tour leader will work as a liaison between the boat crew and his guests to make sure everything runs smoothly and all of his guests are taken care of. Qualified professionals work very hard to make sure that all their clients are properly prepared for the destination, which includes travel to and from the destination, as well as during the trip. They handle all of your booking procedures, and escort you while aboard the ship. Some trips focus on photography or videography classes, others on marine awareness and biology, some are combined with terrestrial and cultural highlights. Whatever the dedicated purpose, make sure it meets your interest. Many professional tour leaders return to their location of expertise year after year, and very possibly know the dive sites as well as the captain (If the captain is new, they may know the area even better) and often know even more about where to find the critters and how to identify them, than the crew does. Since these individuals are with you throughout your trip, they have a vested interest in your comfort and enjoyment. They are very familiar with the overall picture in regards to the destination, airlines, hotel layover stops, vessel range and sea worthiness, local customs, local transportation, best diving seasons, etc... These professional escorts work year round in the diving profession and are accomplished SCUBA professionals with years of experience in dive travel and assisting divers at all levels.

Dive Tour Leader Impostors

With today's ever growing dive travel market, more and more recreational divers are impersonating true professional dive travel tour escorts. These "impostors" arrange for the dive facility and invite their friends and club members to join them on their trip. They sell the spots and promote themselves as the tour leader, but add little, to nothing of a benefit to their paying guests. Few of them have any true diving credentials and have usually little to no professional experience in the industry. They might be photographers, but are generally only interested in their own photos and have no teaching background to assist others. Most of them go about their own business while on the vessel and ignore the group they came with. In fact the only reason they invite others, is so they can reduce the cost of their own trip and can have more to say about the vessel's itinerary. Rarely do they know how to prepare divers for overseas travel and teach them how to deal with rough water conditions, currents, entry and exit techniques, multi-level computer diving, etc. Generally these divers don't retain their income from the dive industry.

How to check up on information you received

• **Magazines**

There are a few non-glossy publications (Undercurrent, In-Depth) which focus on printing unbias advise. These magazines do not support themselves through advertisement, hence allowing their writers to give the reader their honest opinion of the facility, general diving conditions and operation, good or bad. These magazines encourage readers to write and send in their own reviews to be published for all to read. These publications can be of great assistance when researching an unfamiliar destination.

Since most "glossy magazines" are supported by their advertisers, unfavorable reviews are seldom written, due to the simple fact that resorts or boats will not continue to advertise in a magazine that reports negative information. The articles in these magazines tend to be more full of "fluff" then substance. No operation wants to have the magazine include negative information such as: over flowing toilets, rainy weather, poor visibility, etc...

In fact some writers ask the operations' manager what they would like to include or exclude from their article. Seldom will these magazines even carry an article on a destination until they receive enough advertisement money to make it worth the magazines time and pages. "Special Destination Reports" are a way for the magazine to push resorts and Live-Aboards into running ads in their magazine. No one will be excluded if they pay for an ad. If an operation refuses to advertise, the magazine often fails to acknowledge their existence.

Take these so called "reviews" with a grain of salt. Utilize these sources to locate services, along with contact information, pictures and descriptions of a location under **ideal** conditions.

• **On Line Services**

In the the modern age of computers it has become increasingly easier to communicate with a large diving populace through the on-line services. SCUBA diving forums provided by on-line services such as: *CompuServe Prodigy* or *America On-Line*, have become an efficient method of getting up-to-date information on dive destinations world wide. One of the best areas to access, is the forum libraries. Here, you will often find a diver's personal review of a particular destination. If you don't find any information on your desired destination here, you can post a message asking for information on the destination and intended operation you are planning to go with. You'll most likely find several divers to be happy to send you a message with their opinion. Of course, that's their *personal* opinion generally based on their *limited* experience, but if you compare it to the agent's advice and the information you might have found in a magazine or two, you should get a pretty good idea if the travel agent was acting in your best interest.

Can I charter the boat myself and bring my own group?

If your group can take the boat exclusively, then you will generally have more say in the dive site choices and your overall schedule. If booked as an exclusive charter, you may receive a discounted group rate, **but beware...** It is a lot more difficult than one would think to put a group of divers together who will pay on time and not cancel at the last minute...

The minute you mention a dive trip, you will often find lots of divers who *want* to go, but few who will actually come up with the money to *pay* for it. We have met many *"wanna be"* tour leaders who got left holding the bill for spaces they cannot fill. We recommend you leave the organizing to the professionals.

If you have a small group of divers, maybe your family, or just a few friends, and you decide to charter the boat exclusively, it is generally easier to charter a smaller vessel which requires less passengers to fill it. *(One tip for those of you who plan to do this: get your deposits from the divers before you commit to the boat. This will save you and the boat operation from disappointment and financial loss)* Since the numbers required to fill the boat are small, you have a much better chance to fill your spaces so you don't get stuck with unnecessary cost.

Contact Information for :

- Dive Travel Agents
- Direct Bookings
- Professional Dive Travel Escorts/Tour Leaders
- Airlines

Dive Travel Agents

The following are Dive Travel Wholesalers/Dive Travel Agents, who have been in business for several years, and represent several, or all, Live-Aboards around the world. **The listing does in no way constitute a recommendation.**

Adventure Express Travel
650 Fifth St. Suite 505
San Francisco, CA 94107
800-443-0799 415-442-0799 FAX 415-442-0289

Landfall Productions Dive &
Adventure Travel
39189 Cedar Blvd.
Neward, CA 94560
800-525-3833 510-794-1599 FAX 510-794-1617

Poseidon Ventures
359 San Miguel Dr.
Newport Beach, CA 92660
800-854-9334 714-644-5344 FAX 714-644-5392

See & Sea Travel
50 Francisco St. STE 205
San Francisco, CA 94133
800-348-9778 or 415-434-3400 FAX 415-434-3409

Trip-N-Tour Micronesia
846 Williamston St., Suite 202
Vista, CA 92084
800-348-0842 619-724-0788 FAX 619-724-9897

Tropical Adventures
111 Second North
Seattle, WA 98109
800-247-3483 206-441-3483 FAX 206-441-5431

Direct Booking Information

If you prefer to book your trip through the owner/operators of
the vessel, we have listed those who have this service available.
Some of them offer full travel agent services, while others refer
you to a travel agent for your flight arrangements, if requested.

Aggressor Fleet
P.O. Drawer K,
Morgan City, LA 70381
800-348-2628 504-385-2628 FAX 504-384-0817
(All Aggressors)

M/V Ballymena
Out Island Voyages
P.O. Box N - 7775
Nassau, Bahamas
800-241-4591 FAX 809-394-0948

Bilikiki Cruises
P.O. Box 876
Honiara, Solomon Islands
800-663-5363
(Bilikiki, Spirit of Solomons)

Bottom Time Adventures
P.O. Box 11919
Ft. Lauderdale, FL 33339-1919
800-234-8464

Live/Dive Pacific
74-5588 Pawai PL. Building F
Kailua-Kona HI 96740
808-329-8182 FAX 808-329-2627
*(Kona Aggressor II, Palau Aggressor II, Truk Aggressor II,
Fiji Aggressor)*

Peter Hughes' Diving
6851 Yumuri Street #10
Coral Gables, FL 33146
800-9 DANCER 305-669-9391
FAX 305-669-9475
(Sea Dancer, Wind Dancer,
Sun Dancer II, Wave Dancer,
Star Dancer & Febrina)

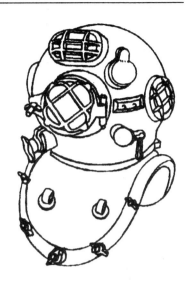

Matagi Princess
Tropical Dive Enterprises
P.O. Box 83
Waiyevo, Taveuni, Fiji Islands
+ 679-880-260 FAX +679-880-274

Mike Ball Adventures
252 Walker St.
Townsville Q. Australia 4810
+077-72-3022 Fax +077-21-2152 800-952-4319
(Spoil Sport, Super Sport and
Telita, New Guinea)

Nai'a
P.O. Box 3179 Lami, Fiji Islands
+ 679-361-382 FAX + 679-362-511

Reef Explorer
P.O. Box 1090
Cairns, Queensland, Australia
+61 70-939-113 FAX + 61-70-939-112

S.S. Thornfinn
Seaward Holidays
P.O. Box DX, Moen, Truk State, FSM 96942
+ 691-330-4253 FAX + 691-330-4253

Professional Tour Leaders

Note: Due to time constraints and lack of responses from some organizations this does not represent a complete and comprehensive list of ALL Professional Tour leaders.

Adventures on Scuba
Tom Campbell
238 Las Alturas Rd.
Santa Barbara, CA 93103
805-965-4951

All Tom's tours include photographic assistance and guidance for amateur shooters as well as for professional photographers and are generally limited to a small group of divers. He schedules his course "A Practical approach to successful Underwater photography" in various exciting destinations.

Aquatic Encounters
Mark Bernardi
1966 Hardscrabble Pl.
Boulder, CO 80303
303-494-8384 FAX 303-494-1202

Mark is a professional tour leader who is extremely familiar with Galapagos, New Guinea and the Red Sea and insures a smooth trip with all details taken care of.

Blue Kirio
Casey Mahaney/Astrid Witte
74-5602 Alapa Str. #764
Kailua-Kona HI 96740
800-863-2524 808-322-4317
FAX 808-322-4021

Astrid and Casey specialize in both, Live-Aboard dive education, ranging from open water courses to underwater photography, and dive tours. Their trips are based on limited participation and emphasize marine identification as well as photography and often include cultural land excursions.

Innerspace Visions
Doug Perine
P.O. Box 557095
Miami, FL 33255
305-669-0118 FAX 305-669-9936

Doug's trips are usually designed to get a small amount of people close to large marine life. Since his trips don't always include comfort and ease, he mostly caters to *"hard core divers."*

Island Explorations
Ann Fielding
P.O. Box 1107
Makawao, HI 96768
808-572-8437

Ann specializes in Dive-Snorkel trips to many remote destinations in the Pacific, with an emphasis on marine-biology. Many of her tours are accompanied by world-renown marine-biologists and include lectures and slide shows.

Jim Church
6744 Crooked Palm Terrace
Miami Lakes, FL 33014
305-824-1833 FAX 305-819-1807

Jim specializes in teaching all Nikonos cameras, including the new RS, as well as video. He conducts tours to many destinations, which always include a course on underwater photography and/or videography. Jim can also be booked through Aggressor Fleet.

Mike Severns Diving
P.O. Box 627
Kihei, Maui, HI 96753
808-879-6596

Mike and Pauline are both marine-biologists who conduct tours on request only. They specialize in very adventurous trips to Indonesia with an emphasis on marinelife.

Rainbow Sea Tours / Chris Newbert and Birgitte Wilms
755751 Kuakini Hwy, Suite 103
Kailua-Kona, HI 96740
800-762-6827 808-326-7752 FAX 808-329-8000

Chris and Birgitte are world renown underwater photographers who escort tours to world class destinations. Their trips are based on limited participation and include an advanced photo seminar with an emphasis on creativity.

Stan Waterman
13 Greenwood Ave.
Lawrenceville, NJ 08648
609-895-1829 FAX 609-895-1873

Stan is a world renown underwater film and video producer. He specializes in teaching underwater video and leads up to eight trips a year on Aggressor Fleet vessels. Stan is a wonderful entertainer and can also be booked through Aggressor Fleet.

Waterhouse Photo Tours / Stephen Frink
P.O. Box 2487
Key Largo, FL 33037
800-272-9122 305-451-3737 FAX 305-451-5147

Waterhouse Photo Tours/Scott Frier
800-272-9122 or 310-390-4258

Scott is a Nikon technical specialist for underwater photography. He writes, lectures and teaches extensively and conducts tours on Live-Aboards worldwide which always specialize on underwater photography. His tours can also be booked through the Aggressor Fleet and See & Sea Travel.

Airlines

Although many travelers prefer to have a travel agent make all the
flight arrangements, we generally prefer to contact the airlines
directly, especially when traveling to remote locations.

ALM Antillean Airlines	800-327-7230
Aeromexico Airlines	800-237-6639
Air Aruba Airlines	800-882-7822
Air Canada	800-422-6232
Air France	800-237-2747
Air India	800-223-2420
Air Niugini	714-752-5440
Air New Zealand	800-262-1234
Air Pacific	800-227-4446
Alaska Airlines	800-426-0333
American Airlines	800-433-7300
Bahamasair	800-562-7661
British Airways	800-247-9297
Cayman Airways	800-441-3003
Continental	800-231-0856
Delta Airlines	800-221-1212
Egypt Air	800-334-6787
Fiji Air	310-670-7302
Garuda	800-342-7832
Hawaiian Airlines	800-367-5320
KLM	800-374-7747
Lacsa	800-225-2272
Malaysia Air	800-233-5597
Mexicana Airlines	800-531-7921
North West Airlines	800-225-2525
Polynesian Airways	800-592-7100
Quantas Airways	800-227-4500
Sahsa	800-327-1225
Singapore Airlines	800-742-3333
Solomon Airlines	800-677-4277
TACA	800-535-8780
TWA	800-221-2000
United	800-241-6522

Arrival and Departure

Arrival

Before you depart for any foreign country, be sure you have the proper travel documents. Many countries only require valid identification, such as a passport, while others may also require a visa.

Transportation arrangements should be made in advance. If arriving on the same day as the vessels departure, most Live-Aboard operations will pick you up or at least arrange transportation to the boat. Be sure the dive  boat has your itinerary before you arrive. This should be done either through your travel agent or directly with the boat itself.

Once you collect your luggage and pass through customs (if applicable) you generally will be greeted by a crew member who will assist you and transport you to the boat.

Note: Whenever feasible, it is a good idea to arrive in some of the more, "off the beaten track" destinations a day or so early. The advantage of this is, to ensure you give any lost luggage items time to catch up with you. It is, at best, an inconvenience to have your luggage delivered to the boat once it has left port, not to mention the possible expense. Often, it is simply impossible once the vessel has sailed from port.

For early arrivals, you will need to arrange hotel and transportation arrangements and/or recommendations from the booking agent.

Travel tip: When traveling in remote foreign countries be advised that the airports are usually small facilities and seldom air conditioned. Few of these places have luggage carts, so moving heavy bags about can be exhausting...Pack accordingly !!!

We travel with an individual luggage cart that will hold up to 75 pounds. This can be carried on the plane and never gets counted as carry-on luggage.

Customs

Clearing customs is generally quite easy. Have your passport and declaration documents handy as you go through. Since we usually have quite a bit of luggage, we always let the custom officials know that we are divers. This tends to answer why we have so much gear and why we came to their country. Since the traveling sport diver is a positive contributor to the local economy, they are often met with welcome smiles.

Since it is common for Live-Aboards to come in and go out on the same day, you might not be able to board the boat until the crew has had sufficient time to clean up. They will usually stow your bags on the vessel and have you board by mid-afternoon to early evening. It's a good idea to take a small bag for any personalized items you might need while waiting. In some places there may even be a half day tour of some point of interest that can constructively kill the time. Most guests usually find a nice shady bar to slowly unwind from the flight.

If you do have extra time, use it to check into whether it is necessary to reconfirm your return flights and how many hours before is required. Most foreign airlines will bump you off a full flight if you don't reconfirm 48-72 hours before departure. Ask the crew or airline personnel before you leave the airport of their policy.

Once aboard, you can settle into your cabin for the duration of the trip. Often divers utilize this time to hook up dive gear and other dive accessories. Expect the Captain to brief all the passengers, on the boat's safety procedures, schedule and diving logistics, once all guest have arrived.

Departure

Since the boat is often leaving on a new trip the day you depart, they will require you to vacate your room early. Some destinations require a 8:00 am departure. If your flight is later in the day, the crew will usually store your luggage until you leave for the airport. Most of the time they will transport you or arrange transport at the appropriate time.

For overseas flights, plan to check in at least 2 hours before flight departure. They **will** bump passengers who don't adhere to this policy. Since facilities can be primitive, it can take a long time to get checked in at a busy third world airport. Patience is often the secret to handling the "slowness" often found in these destina-

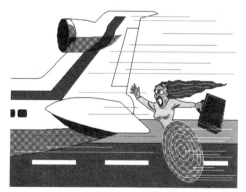

tions. Some still lack baggage x-ray machines, so it is common to have a customs agent hand inspect your luggage. Most of these inspections are to ensure rare artifacts are not removed from the country. If you do find yourself with spare time to kill, checkout the duty free shopping.

Insurance

There are four kinds of insurance all traveling divers should consider.

1) Diver Accident

2) Overseas medical evacuation coverage

3) Trip cancellation and/or interruption insurance

4) Lost baggage

• **Dive Accident and Emergency Evacuation insurance.** All divers should purchase dive accident insurance that covers all diving related injuries and illnesses. This insurance covers recompression and air evacuation cost. Chamber cost can go as high as $20,000 with evacuation cost averaging between $2,000 to $5,000. This insurance is good worldwide.

There are presently two organizations which offer this dive accident insurance and emergency medical evacuation insurance. They are:

Divers Alert Network (DAN) 800-446-2671 or FAX 919-490-6630.

Divers Security Insurance 800-288-4810.

The cost of these programs is under $50/year.

• **Travel interruption and cancellation insurance** is also highly recommended, so that if for some unforeseen reason you can't make the trip, due to an emergency at the last minute, the cost of the trip will be protected. Or, if a hurricane hits the island you are going to and the boat sinks, you will get most of your money back. Check with your travel agent for details on this insurance. It can vary widely so read the fine print.

• **Lost baggage** insurance is usually purchased as a rider on a homeowners policy. The Airlines will reimburse you some money for lost luggage, but it won't be near enough to replace a set of diving equipment, not to mention U/W camera gear. We always hand-carry as much  as we can on the plane. Expensive items such as regulators, dive computers, and any camera equipment is easily placed into a small carry-on bag.

Gratuities

The Live-Aboard dive business is a service industry, and although the general public is seldom aware of it, gratuities are a major part of a crew members' salary. We have found few other recreational activities where the general public relies so heavily on the professionals in charge for their enjoyment and safety.

Besides being at the mercy of Mother Nature, the quality of your experience is based on the people who provide it. A dive-guide can just skip showing a group of divers a point of interest if he chooses to do so. The captain can easily skip a spectacular dive site, and blame it on fictitious weather.

So, if you do have the time of your life, your charter is running smoothly, the service is great, the dive sites are outstanding...don't forget who made it possible....**the crew!** Sure the owners, travel agents, dive shops and anyone else who assisted getting you to the boat helped, but the crew made the difference that really counts.

A good crew will work the boat as if it was the easiest thing in the world, but don't be fooled, it's a tough job. The crew are generally multi-talented and do several jobs on board. Besides providing  the diving part of the trip, they cook the meals, wash the dishes, clean and make up your rooms, stock the bar, monitor the fresh water system, process film (often staying up late at night to finish), and perform the engineering duties that allow for all the comforts of home. The boat is your hotel, restaurant, and dive platform.

"Without a doubt their jobs are service orientated and gratuities are a large part of the crews income."

However, we strongly feel that gratuities should be voluntary and based on the quality of the service the crew provided. If outstanding service is provided, it is not unusual for satisfied customers to tip up to 10% of their charter cost. If you're disappointed with the service the crew provided (keep in mind, it's not their fault, if it rained during your charter), you should inform the manager or captain of your feelings and leave no more of a gratuity than you feel is right. A crew who does a poor job, deserves a poor tip, or no tip at all. You should not reward poor service with a generous gratuity. A very general gratuity guideline we have found to be standard for quality service is: $100-$150 per week of charter per diver.

Dive with the Authors
Blue Kirio specializes in:

-**Exclusive Live-Aboard Dive Training Workshops.** Instructors Capt. Casey Mahaney and Astrid Witte provide simply the very best dive training available. Our individual courses range from a solid beginner's education to workshops on advanced diving skills, underwater photography and marine awareness.

-**Escorted Exotic Live-Aboard Scuba Tours.** All tours are personally selected, prepared and escorted by Capt. Casey Mahaney and Astrid Witte. Travel with us and be assured that you will be getting the **best** of each destination without wasting your time "learning" the area. It takes at least a trip or two, to become acquainted with the local knowledge that is required to turn an average dive trip, into a once-in-a-lifetime adventure. We always "scout" each destination in advance allowing us to include not only remote virgin reefs, but also unique and exciting land adventures.

Blue Kirio offers complete services for the traveling diver. We consider all details of each location and choose all of our tour destinations very carefully, with your **safety** and enjoyment in mind.

All Blue Kirio tours include:

➤ Personalized service, above and below the water
➤ Professional topside and underwater photo assistance
➤ Local marine life familiarization seminar
➤ Land and village excursions
➤ Detailed travel preparation packet on each destination

"Let our years of experience prepare and guide you on your first or next Live-Aboard dive excursion."

To Subscribe to Blue Kirio's free newsletter and travel updates, contact us at:

Blue Kirio
Capt. Casey Mahaney/Astrid Witte
74-5602 Alapa St. #764
Kailua-Kona HI 97640
(800) 863-2524
Tel (808) 322-4317 Fax (808) 322-4021
Email- caseym@interpac.net